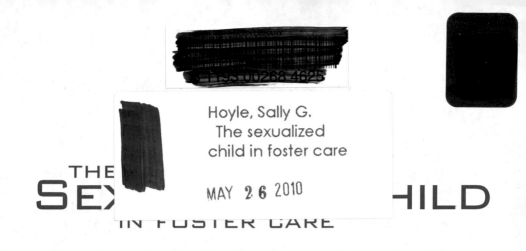

THE SEXUALIZED CHILD
IN FOSTER CARE

A Guide for Foster Parents and Other Professionals

SALLY G. HOYLE

CWLA Press • Arlington, VA

CWLA Press is an imprint of the Child Welfare League of America. The Child Welfare League of America is the nation's oldest and largest membership-based child welfare organization. We are committed to engaging people everywhere in promoting the well-being of children, youth, and their families, and protecting every child from harm.

CHILD WELFARE LEAGUE OF AMERICA, INC.
HEADQUARTERS
2345 Crystal Drive, Suite 250, Arlington, VA 22202-4815
E-mail: books@cwla.org

CURRENT PRINTING (last digit)
10 9 8 7 6 5

Cover design by Luke Johnson
Text design by Sarah Hoctor

Printed in the United States of America

ISBN # 978-0-87868-790-9

Library of Congress Cataloging-in-Publication Data

Hoyle, Sally G.
        The sexualized child in foster care : a guide for foster parents and
            professionals / Sally G. Hoyle.
            p. cm.
        Includes bibliographical references.
        ISBN 978-0-87868-790-9
        1. Foster children--Sexual behavior. 2. Foster children--Mental health. 3. Sexually abused children--Rehabilitation. 4. Child sexual abuse--Treatment. 5. Foster home care. I. Child Welfare League of America. II. Title

HV873 .H68 2000
362.76--dc21
                                                                        99-045584

Contents

Introduction

One of the biggest challenges in foster care today is the increasing number of foster children who have been sexually abused and exhibit severe emotional and behavior problems. In my years as a practicing psychologist working in foster care, I have watched the struggles of foster parents and treatment teams as they work to promote normal development in the midst of severe sexual acting out. Considering the scope of this problem, it is surprising that relatively little is written to guide or inform foster parents and other mental health professionals in treating these children. A review of the scientific literature on child abuse reveals scant reference to foster care. There is a stated view that foster care as a treatment strategy for sexual abuse is inappropriate because the perpetrator should be removed instead of placing the child in out-of-home care [see Lie & McMurty 1991]. The grim reality, however, is that many children in foster care have been abused in multiple ways (emotional, physical, and sexual); have lived in poverty, violence, and chaos; and have mental health problems that are long-standing.

Children in foster care constitute one of the highest risk, yet least understood clinical groups. A survey published by the Foster Family-Based Treatment Association [1996], involving a sample of more than 18,000 children in 221 foster care agencies in the United States and Canada, estimated that 69% of youths in foster care were sexually abused. A different study [U. S. Department of Health & Human Services (HHS) 1997] found that 12% of children entering foster care had a primary problem of sexual abuse. This figure may be a low estimate because sexual abuse is often diagnosed after the child enters the placement. In fact, it is difficult to get a good estimate of sexual abuse in the foster care population, because many national studies combine all types of abuse and neglect (e.g., adding physical abuse, sexual abuse, psychological abuse, and neglect together). It is interesting to note that one national survey on the prevalence of maltreatment in children [HHS 1996] showed that the reported number of sexually abused children has quadrupled, compared with 1980 figures. We can assume that the numbers of sexually abused children in foster care have increased, too.

In a study by Finkelhor, Hotaling, Lewis, and Smith [1990], in which adults were surveyed about childhood abuse experiences, the two highest risk factors were "living in an out-of-home placement" and "living in an unhappy family." Thus, many foster children qualify for both risk factors because their homes could be described as "unhappy." A national survey of current and former foster parents [HHS 1995] cites increasing numbers of children, including those who were sexually abused, as one of the key problems in foster care recruitment and retention today. This report recommends that foster parents receive increased training on parenting techniques with sexually abused children.

The burgeoning literature on childhood sexual abuse and childhood trauma generally neglects the unique perspective of the foster child. Though the adverse consequences of sexual abuse are highly documented, in foster children the effects of sexual abuse are compounded by removal from their normal environment and the people who are familiar to them. Foster caregivers and mental health workers, even those trained in childhood sexual abuse, may find that they are ill-prepared for the intensity of sexual acting out that occurs in a startling percentage of these children. The body of literature on childhood sexual abuse provides us with an understanding of the effects of sexual abuse on a child and his or her family; research and clinical writing on sexual abuse, however, primarily reflects the experiences of children who reside with their birth families. In order to examine the ways in which assessment and treatment of sexual abuse differs in the foster care context, the sexualized child in foster care can be examined from four viewpoints: that of the child, the foster family, the birth family, and the mental health professional.

Unlike the child in an intact family, the child in foster care comes to a family who is likely to lack key information on his or her development. Though obtaining a developmental history is routine in foster care, incomplete information by unreliable parties poses a challenge to assessment and treatment. For example, it is often the case with drug-addicted parents that no family member is available to provide developmental information, or the families are uncooperative because they are angry that the child has been removed. In addition, the child who has been sexually abused may not have made a disclosure. That child is placed in a new home with a family he or she does not know. The family attempts to establish a relationship with the child and to integrate him or her into the family. The child, presumably, makes efforts to get to know the family and to fit in, but may be confused about being in an environment where rules about privacy and sexuality are different. The child begins to act out sexually, and some type of intervention is needed. Two factors, however, can impede assessment and treatment of sexual abuse: the aforementioned lack of knowledge of this child's life experiences and the child's need for time to establish a trusting relationship with the foster family and mental health professionals.

In spite of the need for time to build trust, we also recognize the need for immediate assessment when sexual acting out occurs. Obtaining disclosure may protect the child from further abuse. Thus, the child is taken to meet another unfamiliar person—a social worker, a psychologist, or a psychiatrist—and expected to talk. Children may not talk, and many therapists view this as oppositional behavior or confirmation of severe emotional disturbance. In reality, it makes sense that the child is not talking. We tend to share personal information with people we know and trust, but a child who has been abused has already been betrayed by someone in a position of trust. In addition, the child is in a completely unfamiliar environment and may feel overwhelmed by the number of new people in his or her life.

Unfortunately, difficulties in expressing feelings and escalating behavior problems sometimes lead to the child disrupting the placement. This creates a whole new set of clinical problems, as the child is expected to adjust to even more new people, another school, and different peers, and trust may be even more difficult to achieve.

The foster parents usually have had several hours of training on child sexual abuse. Training tends to emphasize abnormal sexual behaviors to such an extent that even well trained foster parents get confused about what sexual behaviors are normal. Skills of the foster parents dealing with sexualized behaviors vary tremendously, even within a single program where parents receive similar training. Some foster families manage these difficult behaviors well, while others panic easily and need a lot of support. They may not receive training on how their effectiveness in working with sexually acting-out children can be affected by their own past sexual experiences. Sometimes, it is difficult for staff and foster parents to discuss sexuality in an open manner, particularly for foster parents who were raised in a family where discussions of sexuality were discouraged or forbidden. Secretiveness or awkwardness in discussing sexual matters, however, can have a negative affect on the assessment and treatment process.

Foster parent training can be a tremendous help and an important component in placement success. Treacy and Fisher [1993] did a series of studies on foster parent training focused on sexually abused children. First, they gave the foster parents some questionnaires to assess their knowledge and attitudes about sexual abuse. Then they provided foster parents with ten hours of specialized training on normative sexuality, clinical characteristics of sexually abused children, and treatment strategies. After the training, foster parents expressed more confidence in working with sexually abused children and rated the program highly. In another study, Henry, Cossett, Auletta, and Eagan [1991] questioned foster care directors, social workers, and foster parents about sexual abuse training and support for foster parents. Though all of the directors said foster parents were informed about the child's sexual abuse, only half of the foster parents said they had been briefed about the child's abuse status. All participants in this survey agreed that agency staff and foster parents could benefit from more ongoing training on sexual abuse.

Another major concern of foster parents is the highly sensitive issue of foster children who are sexually abused while in foster care. One report estimates the occurrence of sexual abuse while in foster care or adoption at 5.9% [HHS 1996]. When a child is sexually abused in one foster home then moved to a new foster home, the second foster family often has to work harder to establish trust and intimacy. In these situations, foster parents also worry about false allegations of sexual abuse. This will be covered in Chapter 4. The U.S. General Accounting Office (GAO) [1989] reports that nationwide shortages of foster parents can be attributed to several factors, including sexualized behavior in foster children and the possibility of false allegations made by birth parents. Though no statistics were found on false allegations, it appears that children, not birth parents, make the majority of false allegations for reasons that will be discussed later.

Either way, false allegations are a serious concern for foster parents. Foster parents feel vulnerable and open to scrutiny when children begin to act out sexually. They are also faced with balancing the need for the child's confidentiality with the need to instruct family members how to act around a child who is highly sexualized. The foster family may have different cultural values with respect to sexuality than the foster child's family of origin.

Foster parents must also be concerned about the possibility that the presence of a sexualized child might risk the safety of other children in their homes. Foster caregivers often have their own children and/or other nonrelated foster children living with them; it is not uncommon for a foster parent to have three or four foster children in addition to several of his or her own children. Foster parents may also baby-sit for grandchildren, nieces, nephews, or children in the neighborhood. If even one of the foster children is highly sexualized, an environment where children molest other children can quickly develop.

The birth parents of the child face some unique problems, too. They may not have known about the sexual abuse if the child was placed in foster care for other reasons. Often, children display severe behavioral and emotional disorders, and sexual abuse is suspected but not confirmed until they have been stabilized in the safe environment of foster care. This situation can be confusing to birth parents, who wonder why the child did not tell them about the abuse. Though they may have made mistakes in protecting their children, birth parents may worry that their children are being victimized in foster homes. They may themselves be survivors of sexual abuse and may not have received treatment.

Nevertheless, birth parents are frequently absent during therapeutic interventions relating to sexual abuse. Sometimes birth parents are not included because they are perceived as uncooperative. Practical concerns, such as the availability of the birth parents at scheduled appointments, can also interfere with attendance at therapy. Birth parents may not be given basic information about their child. For example, their child may have had a genital exam as part of entrance into the foster care system, which may occur with some agencies if abuse is suspected. If the children are to be reunited with birth families, keeping the families "out of the loop" can contribute to difficulties in both the mental health treatment and reunification process.

Finally, mental health professionals, including social workers, psychologists, and psychiatrists, can also experience difficulty working with the sexualized foster child. As mentioned previously, they are usually working with less historical information that they need. One thing that will help this and many other difficulties is good teaming. This means that everyone on the team communicates regularly around treatment goals for the children. They make efforts to form working relationships that will enhance problem solving.

Few therapists have specialized training in foster care issues, however, and without specialized knowledge, it is easy for crises in teaming to occur. For example, it is a common scenario that the foster parents feel intimidated by the therapist and thus do not share crucial information. Foster parents also perceive that the therapists are scrutinizing them and their child-rearing practices and may become defensive. Therapists may then form negative impressions of foster parents who appear uncooperative. Good teaming will help prevent these types of situations from the start.

Social workers and therapists who work in foster care can also have difficulty staying current on developments in the area of sexual abuse assessment and treatment. Staff can be overextended and caseloads demanding, with little to no time for research and no budget allowance for conferences. Finally, mental health professionals may or may not be trained to monitor their own self-reactions to sexual abuse recovery work, work that can exact a heavy toll personally.

This book addresses concerns of the sexualized child from all four perspectives discussed. It is intended as a practical guide with basic information and training tips for foster parents, therapists, social workers, psychologists, psychiatrists, and other professionals who work with foster children. It reviews the research and clinical knowledge specificially relating to the sexualized child in foster care; also included are reviews from the extensive body of literature on sexual abuse that would be useful to foster parents and mental health professionals who work with foster children. I discuss the developmental needs and normal sexual behavior of the preschooler, latency-aged child (i.e., 6 to 12 years of age), and adolescent; this is particularly important in assessment, because the clinical signs of sexual abuse look slightly different in each age group. References, including journal, book, and Internet resources, are copious for those who seek to go beyond the basics or to focus on a particular topic. Finally, because those who work in foster care tend to be quite busy, I have condensed a large amount of information into bulleted lists for easy reference.

1

Sex and Sexuality

Before we move on to discussions of "normal" sexual behavior in children and assessing and treating sexual abuse, we need to examine our own attitudes about sex and sexuality. Foster children receive treatment from a group of people called a *treatment team* that includes the foster parents, the social worker or case worker from the social welfare agency that removed the child, the social worker or case manager in the foster care agency, the birth family, supervisors of the aforementioned mental health professionals, and perhaps a therapist, psychologist, or psychiatrist. School personnel are included on treatment teams in some settings. Depending on the program, the child is also considered a member of the team. The sheer number of people involved in the treatment of the foster child almost guarantees that there will be differences in how different members of the team approach the issue of sexuality. When team conflicts arise about the treatment of sexually acting-out foster children, team members are often surprised. If you think about it, treatment team members should be expected to have differing attitudes about sex and sexuality. The next section will try to clarify the impact of our own feelings about sex on treatment team functioning and give suggestions on how to resolve these differences.

Attitudes about Sex and Sexuality

It is impossible to totally separate our own feelings and development with respect to sexuality from foster child treatment. We cannot get rid of that part of ourselves, nor should we. The key is to know what your "own stuff" is—that is, your own personal feelings and biases. Individuals who work in foster care need to be able to identify their own difficulties with regard to sexuality and to work with treatment team members in a cooperative way. If you do not, you run the risk of undermining foster care treatment by mistaking normal behavior for abnormal or ignoring an abnormal behavior requiring clinical attention.

Let's start with an example of the ways in which our own attitudes and beliefs shape our interpretations of sexual behavior. On several occasions, a nontraumatized, nonfoster 11-year-old lifts his boxer shorts over his buttocks and smiles provocatively (i.e., a "wedgie"). His 8-year-old brother laughs delightedly and seeks to imitate the behavior. This occurs in the family room in full view of both parents. Though this behavior falls in the realm of "normal" annoying 11-year-old boy behavior, it is not a good idea for one child in a family to expose his buttocks to another child in the name of humor. So the parent then communicates to the older boy that the behavior is inappropriate and why. The behavior then happens infrequently and is met with limit setting. Please take note that, in some families, this behavior would be considered unacceptable due to cultural/religious beliefs, and in some other families this behavior would not result in any response from the parents who view it as a "boys will be boys" type of behavior, again due to cultural reasons.

Suppose an 11-year-old boy in foster care with a history of sexual abuse does the exact same thing. He does the "wedgie" in front of an 8-year-old female foster child who is not his birth sister. She also finds the behavior highly amusing. Is this normal behavior? Well, it depends on a lot of things. How often does this child do it? Does this child do other sexually inappropriate things? Is the behavior done in view of the parents or is it done secretly? How will this action impact the treatment program of the 8-year-old foster child? Does the 8-year-old have a history of sexual maltreatment? These are just a handful of clinical questions a treatment team might ask. It is possible that the behavior is normal, just like the 11-year-old nonfoster child. It is also possible that the child is a sexual abuse survivor and needs treatment.

We will talk later about asking the right questions to make these important treatment decisions. But let's get back to attitudes about sexuality. To work with sexualized children in foster care, it is important for foster parents, social workers, and other team members to examine whether their own feelings interfere with the treatment plan. It is not uncommon for team members to have trouble separating their personal feelings from the clinical treatment of the child. We all have our own sexual beliefs and standards. On any given treatment team comprising three or more people, the likelihood of ideological differences is high. For example, one treatment team faced the pregnancy of an 11-year-old foster child; this case created enormous challenges to teaming due to the diverse feelings of team members on the issues of premarital sex, abortion, and teenage pregnancy.

Training Exercise: Your Sexual Attitudes

To address this issue, it is helpful to reflect on a few key questions that have been adapted from the book *Talking to Your Children About Love and Sex* [Somers & Somers 1989]. Answering these questions yourself or discussing them in small groups will help to increase your awareness of your sexual beliefs and standards.

- What were you told about sex, how were you told, and when?
- Did you get enough accurate information about sex as a young person?
- Do you believe in "women's rights" or do you subscribe to a more traditional role for women?
- How do you feel about birth control?
- Does the threat of AIDS change how you view/teach sexuality with children?
- How do you feel about masturbation?
- How do you feel about homosexuality?
- How much should children know about their parents' sexual relationships?
- Is whatever two consenting adults do sexually their business? How about two consenting adolescents?
- If you could, what would you change about your past sexual behavior?
- How much of any of this would you discuss with your child or foster child?

The topics that are most controversial on foster care treatment teams are premarital sex, masturbation, and homosexuality. It could be a worthwhile training exercise to have small group discussions or role-plays of team meetings that model resolution of conflicts in these areas. Here are two examples of team conflict resolution.

One foster mother was very conservative about sexuality, due to religious beliefs. She had three severely disturbed, sexually abused children. The children were seen by a therapist off and on for six years. The foster mother, who ended up adopting all of the children, prohibited the therapist from talking about premarital sex with the children. The foster mother had some knowledge about therapy with sexually abused children and held the misconception that all therapists condoned masturbation, premarital sex, and birth control. The therapist complied with her request to avoid these topics out of respect for the foster mother's religious philosophy.

The kids, however, got the idea that the way to push mom's buttons was through sex and profanity. The oldest daughter charged hundreds of dollars' worth of calls on a sex phone line, and the kids had sex with each other and were promiscuous with peers in the community. The therapist knew the treatment was affected by constraints in how sexuality could be discussed. It was literally several years into the treatment relationship before the true extent of the sexual acting out was disclosed to the therapist. There was a low level of trust among team members. Ironically, on other issues such as aggressive behaviors, school achievement, and substance abuse, the therapist had a great rapport with the foster mother. The foster mother appeared to like the therapist enough to bring her children to therapy for six years. Yet, the inability to be honest and direct about sex hurt the treatment, and ultimately the adjustment of the children.

In another case, the foster parent had similar, highly conservative views about sexuality; premarital sex was against her religious philosophy. She knew her 16-year-old foster daughter was sexually active and she didn't like it. The same therapist saw this foster child. Though the therapist believed that it is better for adolescents to reach higher levels of maturity before engaging in sex, the therapist also knew from training that sexual abuse survivors often act out in sexual ways and that this was an issue that needed to be dealt with. The therapist was also aware from experience that it takes time to treat this symptom. The team members respected one another's differing positions and developed the following compromise.

The foster mother felt comfortable with designating the therapist and the case manager as the team members to address issues of sexuality. The foster mother asked them to do this in the spirit of supporting the foster mother's ideological stance of abstinence. The case manager and therapist were careful not to usurp parental power and communicated frequently with the foster mother. The foster mother could listen to this material and discuss it with team members, but could not do so with her foster daughter. She acknowledged that her personal history made it hard to parent a sexually acting-out adolescent and sought counsel with friends and parishioners. Team members respected this as her personal business and did not bring it up in meetings, phone calls, or home visits. Openness in handling a sensitive parenting issue enhanced team functioning and, in turn, positive treatment outcomes for the youth.

Now that we have considered our own feelings about sexuality, let's focus on the environment in the foster home. Because we are treating children who have been sexually abused, the next section discusses special considerations related to the needs of these children.

The Sexual Atmosphere in the Home

It can be hard to talk with foster parents about their privacy rules. Foster parents have endured tremendous scrutiny of their background and family to become foster parents. When we discuss the sexual atmosphere in the foster family, the intent is not to intrude or to further scrutinize. The purpose of this section is to suggest that foster parents and team members be sensitive to the concerns discussed below. Here are some questions to think about:

- Do family members keep the bathroom door open or closed?

- Do family members keep bedroom doors open or closed?

- Do children see adults or other children changing clothing in the family?

- Do children see adults or teenagers display affection?

- Do people see one another naked in the family?

It would not be advisable for the treatment team to meet and direct these questions at the foster parents—it could be insulting. However, it is a good idea for foster families and the rest of the treatment team to get a sense about where the family falls on the privacy continuum. In some families, everyone has a lot of privacy and always has clothes on. One foster family called the foster child a "slut" because she did not wear the bathrobe supplied by the foster family. The child was used to different rules. Other foster families are comfortable with nudity. In the latter case, this attitude can cause problems when you are dealing with sexually abused foster kids. So, for example, if the foster family feels comfortable with nudity but has a child in placement who is sexually reactive, then the foster family may need to adjust its privacy customs. This is one of those occasions where private family business becomes a part of the clinical treatment of the child. Good teaming is essential in these circumstances.

Many times we are oblivious to the influences of music, television, videos, and other media on the sexualized foster child. Families are often composed of older and younger children so the younger children listen to adolescent music.

Training Exercise: Music

Get a selection of popular music that the children and teenagers in your community listen to. Listen to the songs as if you are a child who has been molested. Think about how you would interpret the lyrics. Consider the following music and contents:

- "Boom Boom Boom" by the Outhere Brothers, in which there are references to sexual fondling and intercourse.
- "Nice and Slow" by Usher, in which the title reflects the song's theme of preparation and pacing of intercourse.
- "Sexual Healing" by Marvin Gaye, which does not contain as many specific sexual references as the other songs mentioned here, but does portray sex as something a woman does to please a man (i.e., a nonmutual interaction which does not occur in the context of a relationship).
- "Sex and Candy" by Marcy Playground, in which the juxtaposition of sex and candy in the song encourages juvenile appeal for an otherwise adult song.
- "Too Close" by Next, in which there is copious sexual language and sounds as if the singer is simulating intercourse during the song.

Families have different approaches to permissiveness with popular music containing sexual themes. Again, this is a time where the child's clinical treatment will impinge on family customs. If a child is highly sexualized, listening to provocative song lyrics could increase sexualized behavior or cause the child to reexperience trauma by exposure to the sexual stimuli.

Similar concerns exist regarding television. A social worker does a home visit regarding highly sexualized, twin three-year-old girls. The foster mother watches daytime dramas that are filled with sexual encounters and sexualized language. What are the chances of decreasing the girls' sexual behaviors when the television shows give the message that sex is good? Young sexually traumatized children are more likely to decrease the symptoms, in this case "humping" and obscene language, in the absence of sexual models on TV. In this case, the foster mother was advised to watch the programs when the girls napped, or to videotape them for viewing when the girls were asleep. This intervention,

Training Exercise: Television

Watch some television during the day and evening. Watch a combination of dramas, comedy, and talk shows and take note of sexualized behavior and language. Try to view the shows from the perspective of a 7-year-old who is being told not to touch his private parts and to refrain from touching others' private parts. What messages do television shows give? Daytime dramas, talk shows, and many sitcoms teach the following about sexuality:

- People sleep with a lot of people.
- Couples cheat on each other.
- Relationships are disposable.
- Teenagers are highly sexualized.
- The sexier you are, the more people like you.

along with play therapy and good teaming, resulted in decreasing the girls' sexual behavior.

We can make similar observations about movies. Many parents took their children to see "Titanic." This movie contains explicit sexual content and was also too lengthy for even an older child's attention span. Some children enjoy horror movies, which have a lot of sexualized content. Parents let children watch these movies, thinking it is a part of growing up to "get a good scare." Parents may not be aware of the graphic sexuality portrayed in many horror or thriller movies or the depiction of sexual plus aggressive imagery. Generally speaking, movies should be carefully screened for foster children. Foster parents cannot realistically see every movie before their child. Since there are so many movies and the availability changes so frequently, foster parent organizations could develop lists of movies without sexualized and aggressive content, or they could publish parent reviews of the movies.

All this talk about watching what the kids are exposed to in the family brings up an important point. What about respite care? Families who foster acting-out kids may have trouble getting respite care, but they need a break, so they take what they can get. The respite family might then play undesirable music, or perhaps their teenager who shares a bedroom with the child plays it, or they have soap operas on, or they take the kids to a sexy movie. Respite care can really backfire when the child returns home stimulated by sexual material that the foster parents have restricted in their home. There are no easy answers here. Try to negotiate these things with your respite provider without telling him or her what to do. A nice way to present it is to say that part of the child's treatment plan is to minimize sexual stimuli during this crucial part of the child's treatment. Then explain exactly what the treatment team recommends and give specific examples.

What Sexual Information Do You Give Kids—and When?

Foster parents and clinicians are not always sure what sexual information to provide and when to provide it. Though it would be nice to work with the birth parents on this, this is not always possible. The most important thing is to create an atmosphere in your home where sexual concerns or questions can be brought up. Children bring up issues of sexuality pretty regularly if you convey that it is okay to talk about it. For example, a boy comes home and says that a boy in his class said his dad looks at pornography. This can lead to an interesting discussion that would be geared to the age of the child. The following are examples of age-appropriate reactions to this hypothetical situation:

- **The preschooler**: "Some kids' dads look at pictures of people without clothes on. This is not something kids should talk about at school, but tell me if he says it again."

- **The school-aged child**: "Some parents look at pictures and movies of people without clothes on. Some families think this is okay and some families do not. At our house we...(state family philosophy on pornography). It's best if kids don't discuss these things at school, but if it comes up again, let me know. I'm glad you brought this up."

- **The adolescent**: "What do you think about [name-of-child's] dad looking at pornography? It's not illegal to look at porn, but some people find it offensive. They also feel it shows women in a negative way. Do you know how dad and I feel about pornography? Have you ever wanted to look at pornography? What do you guess Dad and I would do if you were looking at some?"

Infants and Toddlers

Experts in sexuality education [e.g., Haffner 1999] suggest that parents begin teaching children about sex when they are infants and toddlers. Sexuality education at this age provides a good framework for teaching children what they need to know about sexuality as they grow up. There are four main issues to address with infants and toddlers.

- **Help them to learn the names of body parts.** Mental health professionals and pediatricians recommend that you teach children anatomically correct names, such as "penis" and "vagina," which do not trivialize body parts. You need to acknowledge that there are cultural differences in traditions about naming body parts. In some cultures, slang names for body parts are customary. Haffner [1999] recommends introducing body part names for genitalia as you teach the other body parts (Here's your nose, here's your tummy, this is your vulva, these are your knees…"). She says this approach teaches infants and toddlers that parents feel comfortable with sexuality and thus do not foster feelings of shame or guilt about their genitalia.

- **Describe what the parts do in simple terms.** For preschoolers, we are talking about explanations like, "This is where the urine comes out" or "This is where a bowel movement comes out."

- **Do some early teaching about who can touch children where and when.** Pediatricians are now trained to make brief comments during children's exams such as, "These are your private parts, and no one except your parents or doctor touches you here." There are many child abuse prevention materials commercially available, even for preschoolers, but they are generally not necessary. Foster parents should consult with treatment team members before involving the child in the use of these prevention materials because they can create unnecessary fear or alarm in some children.

- **Answer questions like, "Where do babies come from?"** At preschool age, it is not necessary to give details about intercourse. Haffner

---

Messages for Preschoolers about Reproduction

- Both a man and a woman are needed to start a baby.
- Babies grow inside a woman in a special place called a uterus.
- Only women can have babies, but men are needed to start a baby, too.
- Mothers can feed their babies milk from their breasts or from a bottle.
- Girls can grow up to be mothers; boys can grow up to be fathers.
- Both mothers and fathers are important to children.

Source: *From Diapers to Dating*, by D. W. Haffner (1999), p. 76. New York: Newmarket

[1999] recommends that preschool children be given the following information about reproduction:

Children Ages 6 to Preteen

At this age, the parents have two functions in sexuality education: to answer questions and to introduce values. Children at this age are now old enough to begin to understand value systems. For many adults, this means teaching the child that sex is an expression of love and caring, not just a way to make a baby. Sometimes answering questions about sex and discussing family values go hand in hand. The following excerpt from *From Diapers to Dating* [Haffner 1999, p. 98] illustrates this point:

> *Parent:* Do you remember when we talked about how babies are made?
>
> *Child:* Yeah.
>
> *Parent:* What do you remember:
>
> *Child:* Something about the sperm and the egg.
>
> *Parent:* That's right. Well, do you also remember that you need a man and a woman to start a baby? In the man, there are special cells called sperm; in the woman, there are special cells called ova. When a sperm cell and an egg cell get together, sometimes a baby can begin. How do you think the sperm and the egg get together?
>
> *Child:* Does the sperm swim across the bed?
>
> *Parent:* That's a good guess. But what really happens is that when grown-ups love each other, sometimes it feels good when the man and woman place the man's penis inside the woman's vagina. After a while, the man's sperm come out of his body and travel up the woman's vagina to her uterus. Sometimes the sperm and the egg come together inside the woman, and that's the beginning of the fetus that will grow into a baby.

As Haffner [1999, p. 102] points out:

> "These simple exchanges can begin to give your child a healthy introduction to sexual intercourse. Answering their questions or providing them with simple information can convey to your children that (a) you respect

Messages for Early Elementary-Age Children about Anatomy and Reproduction

- Male and female bodies are equally special.
- Reproduction requires both a man and a woman.
- Men have sperm cells and women have egg cells in their bodies that enable them to reproduce.
- Intercourse is when a man and a woman place the penis inside the vagina.
- Intercourse is for love, pleasure, and making babies.

Source: *From Diapers to Dating*, by D. W. Haffner (1999), p. 76. New York: Newmarket

their feelings; (b) intercourse is for grown-ups; (c) adults make decisions about when and whether to be involved in sexual behaviors; and (d) in your home, you talk about sexual issues. Not bad for a three-minute discussion!

I would like to add several special issues that need to be addressed with girls and boys at this age. For girls, you need to provide education about menstruation. Menstruation can be a big problem in foster care. Girls act like they know more about feminine hygiene than they actually know. They may have had no training in hygiene or had inappropriate training. Their views of menstruation may be affected by sexual abuse. There are many books available with information on teaching girls about menstruation, which are listed in the resource section. Probably the best strategy for foster families with preteenage girls in placement is to start from the beginning as if teaching a younger child who has not yet had her period. Some parents like to use books or pamphlets on menstruation that can be obtained at reasonable prices from feminine hygiene companies. Some families like to get a "starter kit" from one of these companies, which contains a book and samples of feminine hygiene supplies.

Foster mothers say that there is a lot more to training girls about their periods than the material contained in these educational aids. For example, girls need to be taught the proper way to attend to soiled undergarments and family customs about disposal of sanitary napkins. They need to be taught responsibility for their periods and carrying feminine hygiene supplies when they will need them. They need to learn what to do when unprepared, who to ask, and how to get supplies from the school nurse or a restroom vending machine.

Myths and Misinformation

Can you separate fact from fiction? Below are statements about menstruation. Only one is true. All the rest are incorrect. Can you pick the correct one? Put a check in front of the correct statement. (You'll find the answers below)

○ 1. Drinking icy drinks while you're having your period can make your menstrual flow heavier.

○ 2. Your should avoid strenuous aerobics, horseback riding, jogging, and other forms of rigorous exercise while you're menstruating.

○ 3. You should shower rather than bathe during your period.

○ 4. Eating cold food while you have your period can give you cramps.

○ 5. A permanent wave will not take during menstruation.

○ 6. A woman should not have sexual intercourse during menstruation.

○ 7. If a menstruating woman touches flowers they will wither and die.

○ 8. A woman can't get pregnant during her menstrual period.

○ 9. Stress and lack of sleep can cause you to miss your period.

(Answer: Only statement #9 is true.)

Source: *My Body, Myself*, p. 86, by L. Maderas & A. Maderas [1993]. New York: Newmarket Press.

Another issue that needs to be addressed with school-aged girls and boys is personal safety. Though personal safety is addressed in some parts of treatment, children today need to learn skills for recognizing unsafe situations and what to do if they find themselves in unsafe situations. Girls in particular report experiencing significant amounts of sexual harassment in some school settings. Foster families do an excellent job of teaching girls and boys awareness of how to act in the community with regard to unwanted sexual attention. They teach these skills by example and by describing various problems that could occur along with corresponding courses of action. If you have created an environment in your

---

Training Exercise: Menstruation

For women, discuss how you learned about menstruation. What were you told? What was your reaction to this development? How do girls approach menstruation differently than women who were adolescents 20, 30, or 40 years ago?

---

home where talk about unwanted sexual attention can be discussed, there will be many opportunities to teach children these skills.

Boys are often neglected when it comes to discussing sexuality. Boys need to be taught the basics of sex education, just like girls, and need to be taught about male and female sexuality. Many parents neglect to discuss penis size, circumcision, and erections with boys, which is essential information for boys to be aware of once they start changing into gym clothes in a locker room sometime around the fifth to seventh grade. With sexually abused boys, they might feel something is wrong with their penis if they see another male whose circumcision status is different from their own. If they are taught about the different ways the penis can look, this will prevent needless anxiety. Books on sex and sexuality for children may contain pictures of the circumcised and noncircumcised penis, which would be helpful in teaching this distinction. Nocturnal emissions, or "wet dreams," are another topic often not explained to boys. Again, for a sexually abused boy, it could be quite frightening to have a nocturnal emission if he did not know what it was, especially in light of past abuse experiences. Haffner [1999] recommends telling the boy if he comes across stained sheets to let the parent know or put them where the laundry goes. She also recommends teaching him to do his own laundry.

Training Exercise: Sex & Sexuality Topics for Boys

For male foster parents, discuss the following questions:
- What were you told about sex and sexuality?
- Were you told about circumcision?
- When did you notice differences in the appearance of the penis of other men?
- Did anyone tell you about wet dreams?
- What did you think about this as a child?

What Happens?

Which of these changes of puberty happen only to boys?

○ Gets pimples   ○ Voice deepens
○ Gets wider shoulders   ○ Gets a bigger Adam's apple
○ Has a growth spurt   ○ Grows breasts
○ Makes sperm   ○ Develops wider hips
○ Gets a period   ○ Sweats more
○ Gets hair on the face   ○ Gets greasier hair and body
  odor
○ Gets pubic hair, underarm   ○ Has more sexual thoughts
  hair, and darker leg hair

ANSWER: Only boys make sperm and get bigger Adam's apples
    and wider shoulders. Only girls get a period, grow breasts,
    and develop wider hips. All the other changes of puberty hap-
    pen to both boys and girls.

Source: *Changes in You and Me: A book about Puberty, Mostly for Boys*, p. 42,
          by P. Bourgeois, M. Wolfish, & K. Manyn (1994). Kansas City, MO:
          Andrews McNeal Publishing

Preteens

The foster parent's main function at this age is to continue sex education on a more detailed level. If it is possible to coordinate efforts with the birth family, this would be best. Remember that some children mature earlier, so a "preteenager" may be 9 or 10 years old in some cases.

Many parents begin with a discussion of anatomy and reproduction, including aspects of puberty. Using books and other sexuality education materials, the following topics may be covered, depending on the child-rearing philosophy of the parent: contraception, abortion, sexually transmitted diseases, and sexual orientation. Other aspects of sexual behavior such as abstinence, masturbation, and human sexual response could also be included, again depending on parental values and beliefs. Preteens benefit from conversations about relationships involved in dating and marriage (or other relationship commitments). Some are curious about love and are struggling to distinguish love from other strong feelings. Through these discussions, parents reveal values about sex and sexuality. Teaching about sexual decision making (such as how to say "no") and

Check It Out

I have noticed the following changes in my body (check all the ones that apply):

○ My feet seem to be growing very fast
○ I have noticed vaginal discharge on my underpants
○ I have begun to grow taller at a faster rate than ever before
○ There is more hair on my arms and legs and/or it is darker in color
○ There are curly pubic hairs gowing on my vulva
○ My skin and hair are more oily
○ My breasts have started to develop
○ I have more pimples
○ The skin around my nipples is getting darker in color
○ My hips are getting wider and my body shape is changing
○ I perspire (sweat) more.
○ Hair is gowing under my arms (in the armpits)
○ My body's odor has begun to change
○ I have begun to menstruate

Source: *My Body, Myself*, p. 5, by L. Maderas & A. Maderas (1993). New York: New Market Press

what to do in circumstances involving unwanted sexual attention are recommended. For many preteens, parents will find that they need more than "the talk" or one lecture about sex and sexuality. Questions will arise as they hear about current events (for example, someone in the community caught videotaping up girls' skirts) and social experiences in school (such as what to do about a peer tickling them). As discussed earlier, creating an environment where preteens can feel comfortable asking questions is an important component of sexuality education.

There are many good books in libraries and bookstores that foster parents can use to help them teach these concepts. It is important that the foster parent choose a book consistent with his or her ideology. For example, if the idea of using graphic pictures horrifies you, pick a book without so many pictures. If you want a book with a religious focus, those books are out there. I like the books that have checklists and little exercises the kids can do. These types of books are effective because this format maintains their attention, provides fuel for discussion, and avoids parental lecturing.

I have described several books below, but there is a longer list in the Resources section. You can also obtain a bibliography on sexuality education in the home by writing to SIECUS or using the website listed in the resources section.

- *Changes in You and Me: A Book About Puberty, Mostly for Boys* and *Changes in You and Me: A Book About Puberty, Mostly for Girls,* both by Paulette Bourgeois, Martin Wolfish, and Kim Martyn. These books contain a lot of pictures and are distinguished by having transparent overlays that show body changes. There are lots of quizzes, cartoon-like pictures, "truth and myth," and good anatomical pictures. This book covers everything from "unwanted sex" to homosexuality. It is more liberal than many of the other books. It has an excellent glossary of sexual terms in the back.

- *The "What's Happening to My Body?" Workbook for Girls* and *The "What's Happening to My Body?" Workbook for Boys,* by Lynn Madaras and Area Madaras. These books also have lots of anatomical pictures, lots of question and answer and true and false sections, and fun worksheets. There are quotes by real kids on their feelings about growing up.

- *My Body, Myself,* by Madras & Madras. This is one of the most popular books, probably because there are separate boys' and girls' books with the accompanying workbooks described above. It provides a good overview of puberty, anatomy, menstruation, sexual intercourse, sexually transmitted diseases, and socialization issues.

- *It's Perfectly Normal: A Book About Changing Bodies, Growing Up, Sex and Sexual Health,* by Robbie Harris. This book covers the usual topics about puberty and sexuality using many cartoons and cartoon characters with voice bubbles. It would be especially appropriate for a preteen or teen who would be receptive to cartoon humor.

- *Dr. Ruth Talks to Kids: Where You Came From, How Your Body Changes, and What Sex Is All About,* by Dr. Ruth Westheimer. This mostly narrative book will appeal to parents who prefer to teach sexuality with a minimum of sexually explicit pictures or drawings.

- *How You are Changing,* by Jane Grover. This book, geared for 8-to-11-year-olds is one of six books in a series for the Christian Family called the New Learning About Sex Series. The book emphasizes family values and provides basic information on pregnancy and reproduction.

- *How Sex Works: A Clear, Comprehensive Guide for Teenagers to Emotional, Physical, and Sexual Maturity,* by Elizabeth Fenwick and Richard Walker. This is the only book I reviewed that features photographs of peers to illustrate growth during puberty and social relationships. Some parents might be alarmed by the section entitled "Enjoying Sex." This book contains a comprehensive chart on diseases and infections on pages 82-83.

- *The Period Book: Everything You Don't Want to Ask (But Need to Know),* by Karen Gravelle, Jennifer Gravelle, and Debbie Palen. It has more detail about menstruation than other books reviewed. It discusses other topics, too.

Teenagers

With teenagers, parents should focus on answering questions and discussing sexual decision making. One caution about working with teenagers on having an open dialogue about sex: avoid the "when I was your age" strategy, because the world has changed too much since many of us were teenagers. On the other hand, foster parents can be quite effective in offering advice on topics like sexual harassment and strategies for coping with unwanted attention. Also avoid long, detailed accounts of sexual problems you may have had; most of the children we treat really cannot handle our personal baggage along with their own. Another technique that often does not work can be called the "buddy" technique, where the adult acts like a teenager to gain trust. Inexperienced parents and mental health workers sometimes adopt this approach to achieve intimacy with the youth. The problem is that when you need to discipline the teenager, being in a best friend role is a problem. The best technique to use with adolescents and younger children, however, is being a good listener.

Being a Good Listener

Foster parents and mental health practitioners are often good listeners. Somehow this all gets short-circuited when it comes to sex and sexuality. An adolescent stays out overnight or acquires a sexually transmitted disease, and adults lose their good listening skills and get angry and punitive. The adolescent will then refuse to talk to adults further about sexual concerns. Or she hears the adults on the phone telling friends, coworkers, or supervisors about her staying out all night. Then the adults wonder why the adolescent will not confide in them. Here are some tips:

- **Keep some secrets.** If she tells the foster parent she'll die if anyone else in the family knows she is on birth control and the foster parent tells an adult daughter about it, the foster parent has lied. If you have to tell someone—say, the social worker—you should tell the child/adolescent: "I have to tell [who], because [why]."

- **Try to be natural.** Talking about penises and vaginas should be like talking about the weather. If, for instance, a toddler tells a parent her anus hurts (a common occurrence when they are learning to wipe), the parent should be matter-of-fact about it: "Okay, honey, let's take a look. You need to wipe this way." Use this approach in discussing other sexual matters.

- **Don't interrogate.** Let the child finish telling you what he has to tell you. A boy came home one day to tell his father that a child had been urinating on him in the school bathroom and waggling his penis. It was hard for the father to keep his mouth shut and let the boy finish. Children's stories can be contorted, nonsensical, and lengthy. Hear them out.

- **Be encouraging.** Say things like, "That sounds important." " I'm glad you asked me that." "That's just the right thing for you to do." "Good for you."

- **Don't make the child feel stupid:** "You don't know that? Everyone knows that!" Once, in a foster care girls' therapy group, all the girls agreed that the only time you could get pregnant was during menstruation. The group leaders showed sensitivity in giving the correct information about fertility without making all the girls feel put down. Their response was something like: "Well, you're right that there is one time of the month when you're more likely to get pregnant, but it's *in between* your periods, about two weeks after your period ends."

- **Let the child communicate what he or she wants to say—even if it contains offensive language.** Then recommend different words. "When you are with other kids, you may use the words 'dick' and 'wee-wee,' but with me and Dad, we say 'penis' or 'urine.'"

If your child asks a question at an inopportune time, don't forget to bring it up later! You're in the grocery store checkout with people in front and behind you. Your child asks, "Why are those two men kissing?" or "Why is her tummy so big?" Your answer: "We'll talk about it later, I don't want to make anyone uncomfortable by talking about them." Or you're heading out the door, you're late, and your son says, "Jason showed me his wee-wee." Say, "That's really important for us to talk about, but we need more time to talk. Let's discuss it after supper."

This chapter has introduced us to sexual attitudes and how they affect us. Next, we will look at "normal" and "abnormal" sexual behaviors.

2

What Is "Normal" Sexual Behavior?

Children begin to have sexual feelings as infants, and there is evidence of sexual exploration *in utero* [Sgroi et al. 1988]. When a parent changes an infant's diaper or gives the infant a bath, it is not unusual for the baby to explore his or her genitals. Developmental psychologists and pediatricians agree that infants and young children experience their bodies as pleasurable, and these feelings are part of normal development. Now, talking about sexuality in infants surprises some people. After all, until 15 or 20 years ago, people generally did not talk about sexuality with respect to young children. Sex was something we talked to adolescents about. In some families, sex was not discussed even with teenagers. Sex education was not routine in schools until the 1970s and 1980s. If it existed, it certainly was not presented at fifth and sixth grades, which is now standard in many schools.

It was not until the reporting of sexual abuse increased, which in turn resulted in a substantial scientific literature relating to sexual abuse, that educators, professionals, and parents started to be concerned about normative sexuality. In addition, media images involving depictions of sex and sexual topics have increased and therefore necessitate the introduction of teaching normative sexuality to children early on.

Twenty or 30 years ago, movies and television portrayed little graphic sexuality. Many readers might remember television shows where married people slept in twin beds and intimacy shown on TV was confined to the occasional passionate kiss. There was no reference to sex in the local newspaper or magazines that families kept around the house. In fact, if you look at books written by leading developmental psychologists and pediatricians for parents and for teaching professionals who work with children, there is little mention of normative sexuality. Most parents think they know what is normal when it comes to sex and sexu-

27

ality. Of course, different families have different rules and perspectives on sexuality. Some families allow kids to play doctor, for example. In other families it is forbidden.

Toni Cavanagh Johnson, a psychologist who is an expert in child sexual behavior and abuse, has published a series of materials on normative sexual behaviors that are useful with foster parents and social workers. Johnson distributes her materials at a reasonable cost, and the address to obtain these items is in the references. Foster care providers will find her charts entitled "Behaviors Related to Sex and Sexuality in Preschool Children" and "Behaviors Related to Sex and Sexuality in Kindergarten Through Fourth Grade Children" helpful in distinguishing normal and abnormal sexual behavior. Johnson has also authored the *Child Sexual Behavior Checklist* [1998a], which is described in Chapter 4.

Sexual development can be divided into three categories: infants and preschoolers, school-aged children, and adolescents.

Infants and Preschoolers

Sgroi, Bunk, and Wabrek [1988] describe infants and preschoolers as having an intense curiosity about their own and others' bodies. As they explore the world, they explore their bodies and will learn at a young age whether masturbation is all right, discouraged, or prohibited by their parents. Most children will conform to parental expectations regarding body exploration, looking at other's bodies, and other sexual behaviors.

I would add to this that preschoolers exhibit normative sexual development in their identification as a boy or girl. They tend to ask questions about everything relating to their bodies and are most likely to pose these questions when they are undressing or bathing. Curiosity may extend to "playing doctor" or pretending to have "dates" with same-age siblings or peers. Preschoolers have no notion of privacy unless they are taught privacy conventions. In foster care, some preschoolers who have come from highly undersocialized environments have difficulty with the idea of privacy because it is foreign to them. Preschoolers also enjoy nonsexual touching such as hugs or kisses. They may enjoy touching their genitals, although they will be culturally discouraged to do so in some families.

Socially, preschoolers are learning to have friendships that usually involve gender-divided play. Children may actually play together or side-by-side, which is known as parallel play (e.g., two children playing in a sandbox doing different things with minimal communication with one another). They are learning to understand and label emotions like "happy," "sad," and "mad" (e.g., mad that a peer won't play with them, but happy to go to a birthday party).

School-aged Children

According to Sgroi, Bunk, and Wabrek [1988], developmental game playing is important to school-aged children (6 to 10 years). Children this age may continue to self-touch and to seek opportunities to see another child's genitalia, though more in a play contact, like "hide and peek" or "playing doctor." Sometimes there is a competition aspect, like seeing who can urinate farthest. Again, adults in the child's life are likely to influence the practice of these behaviors.

In my practice, I have noticed that in school-aged children, roughly 6 to 12 years of age, gender roles are more defined. They are likely to ask questions about reproduction and to want more details. School-aged children have well-developed conceptions of privacy, and their privacy needs increase during this age range. They may not want an adult present when they are changing clothing or bathing. Children may touch their genitalia and may do so in front of others. If self-touching is allowed in the family, they may be more deliberate about masturbation. Sex play continues in this developmental age and is likely to be of the "I'll show you mine, you show me yours" variety. If children are not supervised, as is true in neglect cases, a lot of this type of play can occur among siblings.

Socially, the school-aged child is learning to make more sophisticated decisions. Friendships continue to be mainly with the same gender. They may have a "crush" on a child of the opposite sex, which typically does not involve sexual feelings. The 6-to-12 crowd watches more TV and listens to more music than the preschooler and may respond to inappropriate sexual models by verbalizing or imitating these behaviors. They learn inappropriate words from TV, music, and videos, as well as from peers. They may begin to ask about heterosexuality and homosexuality. If parents are single or divorced and engage in dating, the latency-aged child is bound to have questions pertaining to social relationships.

Preadolescent and Adolescent Years

Sgroi, Bunk, and Wabrek [1988] describe children in the preadolescent and adolescent years as influenced by bodily changes that accompany puberty and social stimuli, such as music and television. Masturbation is described as a normal sexual behavior, though many families do not agree with this notion. Socializing becomes important, starting with same-age peer groups and evolving in adolescence to dating behaviors. Sexual interactions may or may not be a part of adolescence. For many adolescents, this may consist of kissing and fondling activities but can also involve sexual intercourse.

Though we have spoken about the 6- to 12-year-olds, there are a few particular things to say about preteenagers, a group with an age range that can span from 9 or 10 to 12, depending on physical and psychological maturation. Preteens have questions about puberty and may be embarrassed to ask. It can be tough to be either an early maturer or a later maturer. Preteens are very sensitive about their appearance and worry that people are looking at them. Socially, there is a shift to reliance on peers rather than parents, and they tend to vacillate between dependence and independence. They begin to identify with a particular social group such as kids who like computers, shopping, or certain music. Some preteens explore heterosexual relationships by talking on the phone or "going together." They may kiss but, in the majority of cases, physical contact does not go beyond that.

Teenagers experience rapid growth, skin changes (i.e. pimples), and an increase in sexual thoughts and feelings due to hormonal development. They fantasize about relationships with movie stars, musicians, or an older peer or adult. Teens worry about their appearance, but the worries are more extensive than the preteen: "Are my breasts (or penis) big enough?" or "Why don't I look like a famous actress or actor?" Their privacy needs increase dramatically, and parents struggle with balancing their "need to know" and the child's privacy. Their cognitive development allows them to consider more complicated notions of love, such as how to know when you are in love. They have questions about sex, sexually transmitted diseases, and contraceptives, depending on their social context. Sexual orientation develops during the teenage years, though many individuals report being aware of their sexual orientation earlier in their development.

Socially, teens start out interacting in mixed-sex groups and gradually make the transition to dating. Dating becomes a big social focus. There is an interest in kissing and mutual touching, and in some teens, intercourse. Teenagers can be moody and confused and consider peers to be more important than parents.

What Is Not Normal?

Johnson [1991] presents a useful list of circumstances to aid parents and mental health professionals in determining if sexual behaviors are normal. I have expanded Johnson's original list, using examples specific to foster care:

- The child has greater sexual knowledge than do other children his/her age. A three-year-old foster child who uses adult sexual language and has sexual knowledge comparable to a much older child is a good example. The child does not just repeat words relating to intercourse, but also has some rudimentary knowledge of what they mean.

- The child is overly interested in sex to the exclusion of other activities. One six-year-old foster child was preoccupied with adults and teens of the opposite sex. He was careful about his appearance and enjoyed watching women instead of playing.

- The child is involved in sexual interactions with children who are much older or much younger. When a ten-year-old exposes himself to a three-year-old, it is not normal sex play. A seven-year-old boy who interacts with adolescents in a sexualized manner, like hanging out on the street making comments about girls walking by, is not normal.

- The child engages in sexual activities with children he/she does not know well. A foster child who is in a store with the foster family and tries to pull down another child's pants is not normal.

- The child uses bribes or force to engage in sexual behaviors. As will be discussed in Chapter 6, children who molest other children may bribe other children with candy. Alternatively, they may threaten the child or members of the birth or foster family in order to gain compliance with sexual activities.

- The child has ideas about sex that do not make sense. One eight-year-old foster child who sexually victimized his four-year-old foster sister, when caught, said, "She wanted me to do it."

- The child manipulates others to touch his/her genitals or hurts his/her own or other's genitals. For example, a seven-year-old child straddles her legs and places a toy on her crotch, beckoning to a three-year-old sibling to get the toy.

- Other children complain about the child's sexual behaviors. Even young children recognize sexually inappropriate behaviors and complain about them to foster parents.

Preschool and Early-Elementary Sex Play: Harmless or Problematic?

Here's a quick way to assess whether childhood sex play is likely to be harmless or whether you should be concerned:

	EXPECTED	PROBLEMATIC
Ages of Children	Similar	More than 3 years
Children Seem	Giggly, curious, happy	Aggressive, angry, fearful, withdrawn
Activities	Undressing; playing doctor or "You show me yours, I'll show you mine"	Oral, anal, or vaginal intercourse; penetration with fingers or objects
After Discussion with Parents	Behavior stops	Behavior continues

[Haffner, 1999, p. 60]

- The child continues to exhibit sexual behaviors when told by an adult to stop. As mentioned earlier, most children want to please adults, even those in a new foster home. If foster parents repeatedly tell a child to stop sexual behaviors and they do not, this is a red flag.

- The child appears nervous when sexual issues are brought up. A normal child who has participated in sex play with a same-aged peer is likely to admit to it and may feel embarrassed. They are not likely to seem uncomfortable when the adult raises this or other sexual issues.

- The child exhibits strange toilet behaviors. Two foster brothers, ages three and six, were intent on seeing their foster mother undressed or using the bathroom. Children who spend lengthy periods of time in the bathroom masturbating should also cause concern.

- The child's drawings show genitals as a focal point. Some foster children draw themselves or family members with prominent genitalia or tell adults that genitalia are missing from pictures they see others draw.

- The child engages in sexual activity with animals. There have been cases of foster children "humping" a family dog or placing a cat in their lap in a sexualized manner. Children may also attempt to digitally penetrate an animal. These behaviors are not normal.

- The child has frequent erections or vaginal discharge. One foster adolescent was observed by his foster mother to have frequent erections to a degree that was apparent to her and school personnel. Many foster parents notice that their foster daughters have an odor that they cannot identify, possibly with vaginal discharge. All of these types of concerns need to be investigated for health reasons.

Sex Between Siblings

Sex between siblings is a concern that is often overlooked in conducting sexual abuse assessments with foster children. In foster care, children are typically placed with siblings if possible. We want to preserve this support system and decrease the unfamiliarity of an already strange transition. These birth siblings are often blended in a foster sibling group that includes children of the foster family, child relatives of the foster family, or friends' children who are being raised by the foster family. The research literature shows some normative amounts of sexual activity among siblings [see for example Finkelhor 1981] described by college students; 15% of females and 10% of males described some type of sexual touching with siblings. By "normal" amounts of sexual activities, popular examples might be playing doctor or showing one another genitalia on a limited number of occasions.

Research on sexual abuse has not investigated sibling sexual activity between siblings in foster care. But anyone who works in foster care knows it happens. The book *Sibling Abuse: Hidden Physical, Emotional, and Sexual Trauma* by V. R. Wiehe (see Resources section) does not mention the issue of sexual abuse in out-of-home care at all, but it does offer a comprehensive clinical description of the problem in general, with copious clinical examples if you wish to read further on this topic. Poland and Groze [1993] surveyed foster parents on the effects of foster care placement on their children. Parents expressed concerns that their foster child would be abused by other foster children in 10% of the sample.

Clinical experience indicates that, in children with highly sexualized behavior, the likelihood of sexual interactions among children in the family—foster or nonfoster—is higher than for nonabused children.

It is also the case that the foster child may not have disclosed abuse, and when the family and treatment team are lacking this information, they have no reason to provide the extra supervision that would be required. Sometimes team members are reluctant to admit that one child is molesting another. This will be discussed further in Chapter 6.

Now that some of the "red flags" in children's sexual behavior have been outlined, it is time for a more detailed discussion of the signs and symptoms of sexual abuse.

3

Signs and Symptoms of Sexual Abuse

This chapter describes the signs and symptoms (both behavioral and physical) of childhood sexual abuse, the effects of sexual abuse, as well as the different types of sexual abuse. Remember as you read this chapter that virtually all of the research that has helped us to understand sexual abuse is based on children who are not foster children. Though foster children present symptoms that are similar to nonfoster children, foster parents may have children placed in their homes years, months, or days after the child was abused. This presents a challenge to clinical teams, who do not have the advantage of observing the child over a period of time; in addition, it is often weeks or months into the placement before sexual abuse concerns become evident.

It is useful to note the prevalence and incidence of sexual abuse in the general population of children before we move on to specifics. Finkelhor [1981] conducted a survey of 800 college students, which included questions about childhood sexual experiences. Based on this questionnaire, and defining sexual victimization as a sexual experience prior to the age of 12 with an individual at least 5 years older than the respondent, Finkelhor estimated that 19% of females and 9% of males have been sexually abused. The extensive research of Finkelhor and others has shown that sexual abuse is not confined to any particular age, gender, race/ethnicity/culture, socioeconomic status, or physical location (for example, rural versus urban).

As we proceed with this discussion, keep in mind that not all children who display the symptoms below have had physical contact with a child sexual abuse perpetrator. Remember, too, that sexualized behaviors in children can occur in the absence of a sexual abuse experience. Families may allow young children to view adult material on television and in the movies, may be relaxed about nudity, or the household may be so chaotic that the child is exposed to adult sexuality. Some children who sexually molest others do not have a history of abuse. (Child offenders will be discussed in Chapter 6, in the context of sexually aggressive children in foster care.)

Sharing Information

I need to make one important point before we examine the signs and symptoms of abuse. Foster parents *must* be informed prior to placement about assessment information, to provide appropriate supervision, and to function as a part of the treatment team. In one research study, program personnel said they told all foster parents that the children had been abused, but only half of the foster parents recalled being given the information [Henry et al. 1991]. Now it is true in some cases that foster parents are not given this information. This can happen for several reasons.

First, it may be that details about the abuse are not yet known; as they are known, they need to be shared with the foster parents. For example, one foster child behaved in sexual ways and urinated on the floor. The foster parent could find no traditional discipline method to stop this. The child had play therapy, and the therapist asked a series of questions designed to understand the urinating behavior. The most important question the therapist asked was, "You have been peeing in places that are not the toilet. Do you know anyone else who pees in places that are not a toilet?" The child responded positively and stated that an acquaintance of her birth mother had urinated in her mouth. The therapist and foster mother then discussed what to say to stop the urinating on the floor. They agreed to tell the child that this man had made a mistake peeing in her mouth and had gotten her mixed up about where to urinate. They told her that in this family, people only urinated in the toilet and she would need to do the same. The behavior stopped almost immediately with this team effort. Suppose the therapist had not shared this information with the foster mother—the symptom would have likely continued.

Foster parents may not receive the information on the child's sexual abuse at placement because the person doing the placement wants to protect the foster parent from hearing the grizzly details, or thinks maybe the foster parent could not "take it," or has concerns about the foster parent maintaining confidentiality. They should remember, however, that foster parents are professionals who have been trained to manage the difficult and troubling case histories of the children they foster. They have also been trained in confidentiality. They need the information to effectively parent the child.

Finally, foster parents may be told the details about the abuse but do not retain the information because it is upsetting to them. If this is the case, further training may need to be done around this issue.

Withholding information can be a two-way street. There are some instances when the foster parents do not report sexualized behavior in the home because they are worried that program personnel will think they are not good parents. Some parents do not tell the others on the team because they feel like they are "telling on" the child, getting him or her in trouble, or revealing embarrassing personal material that might upset the child. Others do not share sexual information simply because it makes them nervous to bring up the whole topic of sex in a room full of people on the team. Finally, withholding of information can occur when there is poor teaming and the foster parent is distrustful of other team members. The information needs to go both ways for assessment and treatment to be effective.

Based on a review of research, I have developed a list of general signs and symptoms of sexual abuse for children of all ages from several sources [Kendall-Tackett et al. 1993; Kinnear 1995; Walker et al. 1988; Browne & Finkelhor 1986]. Please keep in mind that one of the challenges of child sexual abuse assessment in foster care is the lack of information on the child's functioning prior to placement. For example, children who are abused may display school problems, but foster care staff may not have information on the child's prior school adjustment. Sleeping and eating problems are hallmarks of sexual abuse, but in chaotic, poverty-stricken families, bedtimes and mealtimes may not be regular. It may be hard to judge "problems" in these areas for these children. Another important thing to remember before you review the lists below is that Kendall-Tackett and colleagues [1993] found that no particular symptom on the list occurred in all child abuse survivors except symptoms of posttraumatic stress disorder (PTSD, described in the following section). Other symptoms on the list occurred in 20% to 30% of abused children. Then there are a proportion of children who are sexually abused and show none of these symptoms when assessed on the instruments used in the research.

General Signs and Symptoms

- Posttraumatic stress
  - recurrent thoughts of the abuse, which may be acted out in play
  - bad dreams about the abuse
  - "flashbacks" of the traumatic event
  - distress at things that remind the child of the abuse and/or physiological reactivity to similar situations
  - avoiding or forgetting aspects of the abuse
  - being detached, disinterested, unfeeling, and hopeless about the future
  - sleep problems, trouble concentrating, watchful or easily startled
- Sexually inappropriate behaviors
  - bizarre, sophisticated, or unusual sexual knowledge for child's age
  - seductive or promiscuous behavior
  - excessive masturbation (note that some religious or cultural orientations consider any masturbation to be abnormal)
- Regressive behaviors
  - enuresis (bed wetting)
  - encopresis (fecal soiling)
  - tantrums, whining, clinging
- Runaway behaviors
- Aggression/cruelty
- Depression
- Delinquency
- Self-injurious behavior
- Withdrawn behavior

Behaviors that are less frequently reported include the following:
- Eating problems
- Pregnancy or sexually transmitted diseases
- Overly compliant, overachiever, too responsible

Signs and Symptoms by Developmental Levels

Though the preceding list is helpful, there are some signs and symptoms particular to children of different ages. If you have a child who is mentally retarded, you would want to look at that child's developmental level of daily functioning and refer to that list. For example, if you have a 10-year-old foster child who cognitively and socially functions like a 4-year-old, that child is more likely to display symptoms of sexual abuse commonly seen in the preschooler.

Preschoolers

- Anxiety
- Nightmares
- Symptoms of posttraumatic stress disorder
- Inappropriate sexual behavior: sexual behavior toward peers or adults (such as touching adults' genitals), inserting objects in vagina or anus
- Depression/withdrawal
- Acting out behaviors

Symptoms that are less frequently reported include the following:

- Fearfulness
- Urinary or bowel problems, toileting problems
- Bleeding, discharge, reddening, or odor from sex organs
- Regressive behaviors (clinging, acting like a younger child)
- States he/she was abused ("He touched my pee-pee"), reenacts abuse in play (for example, pretends dolls or action figures are having sex)

School-Aged Children

- Symptoms of posttraumatic stress disorder
- Excessive fears (for example, the child does not want to go home from school or arrives early and stays late)
- Aggressive behavior
- Hyperactivity
- Nightmares, sleep disturbance
- School and learning problems (such as grades dropping)
- Regressive behaviors
- Depression

Behaviors that are less frequently reported include the following:
- May discuss abuse, but also likely to separate feelings from event (i.e., isolation of affect)
- May reenact in play
- Low self-esteem
- Running away
- Eating problems

Adolescents
- Depression: withdrawn, suicidal, self-injurious behaviors
- Posttraumatic stress disorder
- Somatic complaints (e.g., headaches, stomachaches)
- Illegal acts, delinquency
- Running away
- Alcohol/substance abuse
- School and learning problems

Teenage behaviors that are less frequently reported include the following:
- Promiscuity, in some cases prostitution
- Overly compliant behavior
- Eating problems, eating disorders
- Negative self-image
- Guarded, suspicious

One research study examined the effects of sexual abuse in foster children of different developmental levels by administering questionnaires to foster parents. Thompson, Authier, and Ruma [1994] asked foster parents to respond to questionnaires about adjustment. The results summarized here are the problem behaviors that foster parents noted as occurring "frequently" or "sometimes" by at least 50% of the foster parents filling out the questionnaires.

For preschoolers, foster parents reported that unreasonable fears, seductive behavior with peers, nightmares, eating problems, aggressive behavior, sleep problems, and clinging behavior were the most problematic. Preschoolers were most likely to show aggressive behavior (80% of respondents) and clinging behavior (70% of respondents). Preschoolers are also more likely to masturbate and expose themselves than children of other ages, according to this study. This is important information for new foster parents who anticipate fostering the young, sexually abused child. Often, foster parents have the perception that these children will be easier to handle than the older child. They are likely to need close supervision, however, and can have a lot of behavioral and emotional concerns.

For the 6- to 10-year-old age group, Thompson and colleagues found that the largest number of problem behaviors included bed wetting, unreasonable fears, seductive behavior within the foster family, seductive behavior with peers, nightmares, eating problems, aggressive behavior, physical complaints, school problems, sleep problems, and clinging behavior. These results are consistent with a study of nonfoster children, which demonstrated the highest levels of clinical psychopathology in children ages 7 to 13 [Gomes-Schwartz et al. 1985]. The problems that yielded the highest number of foster parents responding were eating problems (96%), clinging behavior (85%), and nightmares (80%).

The children in this age group are also prone to runaway and suicidal behaviors, may exhibit self-mutilation, or engage in drug/alcohol abuse at an early age. Foster parents need to know that the 6- to 10-year-old age group may in some ways be the most difficult to foster because they display the highest number of symptoms as a group. Remember that every child in this age group will not show all of these problems, and they can vary in severity from child to child.

The 11- to 13-year-old group had fewer behavioral and emotional concerns in this study, as was true in the Gomes-Schwartz et al. [1985] study. Nevertheless, the following behavioral problems were noted for this age group: unreasonable fears, seductive behavior with peers, nightmares, eating problems, physical complaints, school problems, sleep problems, and clinging behaviors. Most problematic in this group were eating problems (79%) and school problems (74%). Like the 6- to 10-year-old group, the 11- to 13-year-olds are also likely to engage in suicidal behaviors and self-mutilation, according to foster parent responses.

Finally, teenagers fostered by the parents who completed the questionnaire had a slightly different list of concerns: seductive behavior with peers, promiscuous behavior, nightmares, eating problems, aggressive behaviors, physical complaints, school problems, and sleep problems. Highest ratings were given to school (78%) and sleep (72%) problems. Teens are also seen as engaging in suicidal behaviors and are at risk for drug/alcohol abuse. The one behavior that distinguishes the adolescents from the other age groups is promiscuous behavior, which can lead to many other problems. In foster care programs, difficulties with teenagers being out overnight or past curfew often relate to promiscuous behavior. Teenagers who are sexually active are at risk for sexually transmitted disease, teenage pregnancy, and sexual assault.

Physical/Medical Signs of Abuse

There are some important physical signs and symptoms associated with child sexual abuse that foster parents and clinicians need to be aware of. Keep in mind that the physical problems listed below must not be attributable to another condition. For example, a child may fall on his or her bicycle causing genital discomfort, have pain urinating due to a bladder infection, or have vaginal itching due to a yeast infection. All these circumstances are not uncommon in childhood.

Veltkamp and Miller [1994] list the following physical symptoms associated with sexual abuse:

- Trouble walking or sitting
- Bruises or bleeding in the mouth, anus, or genitalia
- Torn, stained, or bloody underwear
- Pain while urinating
- Vaginal or penile discharges
- Semen on clothing
- Pregnancy or sexually transmitted diseases (STDs)
- Complaints of pain, itching, or irritation of genitals
- Somatic complaints/chronic ailments with no known etiology

These physical symptoms are things foster parents want to especially notice when the child is first placed in care. Sometimes it is not yet known that the child has been abused, and the medical symptoms can be the first clue that the child has been sexually abused. Typically, by the time a child is placed in foster care, all or many of these symptoms may have abated. If the child has a sexually transmitted disease, however, symptoms will persist. It is sometimes the case that children cause chafing to the genital area by vigorous masturbation, and this has been a concern among many foster parents. In addition, foster parents of sexually abused children commonly report constant complaining about physical ailments in the absence of a known medical condition (i.e., somatic complaints).

Types of Sexual Acts Perpetrated on Children

It is helpful to know something about how the child was abused to provide proper assessment and treatment. Several authors who write about sexual abuse, such as Veltkamp and Miller [1994] or Hobbs et al. [1993], provide a list of the types of sexual abuse perpetrated on children. Though presentation of this list may make some people uncomfortable, when children disclose sexual abuse, foster parents and mental health professionals need to be aware of what sexual acts constitute abuse.

Sexual Abuse with Physical Contact
* Sexualized fondling, touching, or licking of child, including:
    - touching a child's genitals or breast
    - inserting finger or objects in vulva or anus
    - masturbating in front of child
    - rubbing penis on child or between child's legs (the latter is referred to as intracural intercourse)
* Making the child sexually fondle the adult
* Vaginal, anal, or oral intercourse
* Rape
* Prostitution (defined as any of the above that also includes an exchange of money, gifts, or favors, and applies to both boys and girls) [Veltkamp & Miller 1994]

Sexual Abuse Without Physical Contact
* Exhibitionism (e.g., flashing)
* Photographing or videotaping the child naked for use in pornography
* Showing the child pornographic material
* Erotic or sexually explicit talk
* Sadistic activities involving children
* Burning a child's buttocks or genitals

One confusing aspect of sexual abuse for some parents and mental health professionals is the fact that some forms of sexual abuse are not perceived as harmful, but rather pleasurable to the child. If the abuser does not hurt the child and presents sexual experiences in a playful manner with positive rewards such as attention, food, or candy, the child does not feel "abused." He is confused when foster parents or mental health professionals talk about him "getting hurt" or "bad touching," as it wasn't "bad" for him.

Effects of Sexual Abuse on Foster Children

The general signs and symptoms discussed earlier pertain to the child's initial reaction to sexual abuse. Browne and Finkelhor [1986] define short-term effects of childhood sexual abuse as reactions that happen from the time of the abuse until two years later. Long-term effects refer to reactions that occur more than two years after the abuse. In foster care, it is difficult to draw the line between short-term and long-term effects. Many foster children are abused for periods of years in multiple ways. We may not know when the abuse started and may have no reliable way of finding out. Since children in foster care have shorter lengths of stay now than in the past, I have focused in detail on short-term effects, which are likely to occur while the child is in care. I discuss the long-term effects briefly here.

Long-Term Effects

- **Depression.** Adults molested as children most frequently describe depression as a problem.
- **Self-destructiveness.** Adult survivors of sexual abuse are more likely than nonsexually abused adults to make attempts at self-harm (e.g., suicide attempts) [Browne & Finkelhor 1986].
- **Anxiety or tension.** Anxiety or tension in adult survivors of abuse is manifested in anxiety attacks, sleep problems, nightmares, and eating disorders.
- **Dissociation** (e.g., "out of body experiences" or "spacing out").
- **Feelings of isolation and low self-esteem.**
- **Juvenile delinquency.** Widom and Ames [1994] found childhood sexual abuse survivors were more likely to be involved in juvenile criminal activities and running away from home compared to other types of abused and neglected youths.
- **Susceptibility to further abuse.** Some research shows that adults abused as children have a higher likelihood of being sexually victimized. In children, studies show that the rate of reabuse is 6% to 19% of children [Kendall-Tackett et al. 1993].

- **Trouble with sexual functioning**.
- **Substance abuse**.

Please keep in mind that not all children who are sexually abused experience long-term effects. Also, individuals who experience long-term effects are unlikely to have all of the symptoms listed above. It is also the case that the child's preabuse functioning affects how he or she manages other abusive events that may occur in the future, as well as the extent to which the child exhibits long-term effects [Briere & Elliott 1994]. Factors that could affect preabuse functioning are temperamental differences, history of other psychological disorders, and quality of attachment and bonding with the primary caretaker. We all have known children in foster care who seem immune to the horrendous environment, poor caretaking, and instability in their lives. Other children are easily debilitated by a similar environment and/or trauma.

How Mental Health Programs May Exacerbate the Problem

Though the intent of the mental health system is to protect children from harm, there are some aspects of the process of sexual abuse assessment that contribute to the effects of the abuse itself.

- Mental health personnel may alienate children and/or foster parents or other team members.

- Repeated interviewing is upsetting for the children and can lead to increased acting out, which negatively impacts the foster family.

- The physical exam for sexual abuse may traumatize the child. Sometimes exams are repeated because they are first examined as part of the initial screening process in foster care by a physician who may not be specially trained in sexual abuse diagnosis.

- Longer lengths of stay in foster care due to lengthy court proceedings may have a negative impact.

- Court attendance itself can be traumatizing. In some states children's testimony is videotaped, but in many states children must still face their perpetrator in court. Emotional risks to the child can be minimized by resolving cases in shorter periods of time, ensuring that the child does not testify repeatedly, and by using videotaped testimony so the child need not be traumatized further [Kendall-Tackett et al. 1993].

- Withholding of sexual abuse treatment or excessive, inappropriate treatment for sexual abuse.

Now that we have examined the signs and symptoms of sexual abuse, we need to understand how professionals make assessments that the child has been sexually abused.

4

Assessment of Sexual Abuse

The assessment of sexual abuse can be a tricky business. If the mental health professional doing the assessment is wrong, the consequences could be severe. If the assessment shows that the child was not abused, but in reality the child was abused, it could lead to the child being discharged to a family in which the child will be unsafe from further abuse. On the other hand, if the assessment shows that the child was abused and is wrong (e.g., a false allegation of abuse by the child), a child may be wrongfully kept from his or her family, and family members may face criminal charges when they have done nothing wrong. The good news is that there is an enormous amount of clinical and research literature on the assessment of sexual abuse, including how to conduct investigations. This chapter presents highlights of this literature.

How Reliable Are Children's Reports?

When a child returns home from school, parents routinely ask how the school day went and what occurred during the day. Parents of school-aged children can tell you that they rarely get an accurate report about the actual school day. A child is likely to report a problem (such as physical injury or a lost tooth), to be vague or illogical, and to omit important details. Experienced parents know if they ask the right questions and know the child's school routine (such as, "Whose turn was it to do the calendar?" or "Did you have your spelling test?"), they get more of the information they are seeking.

In developing techniques of interviewing children about child abuse, professionals have taken into account this knowledge about child development. Successfully eliciting accurate child abuse information from children is a special skill affected by numerous factors.

- **Age of child**. Obviously, older children have better verbal skills with which to report sexual abuse. Older children are less susceptible to suggestibility than younger children in research studies. If the interviewer said, "He touched you there, didn't he?" a younger child is more likely to say "yes" than an older child is, regardless of whether it were true. The interviewer should ask nonleading questions like, "Where did he touch you?" Here's another example. If a 3-year-old ate a peanut butter sandwich right in front of her preschool teacher, and later the teacher said, "You didn't have a peanut butter sandwich for lunch, you had a turkey sandwich," the 3-year-old is more likely to go along with the adult than a 10-year-old.

- **Specificity of details**. The younger the child, the more cautious you need to be in asking for details. Young children lack the cognitive skills to determine time, date, and location of an incident. Older children are more capable of providing details.

- **Interviewer's position of authority and interviewing style**. It has been found that children who are interviewed by an authority figure are more susceptible to suggestibility by the interviewer [Kuehnle, 1996], and most adults are viewed by children as authority figures. When the interviewer approaches the child in a supportive manner, however, the likelihood of the child acquiescing to a misleading question decreases. Successful interviewers adopt a style in which they appear interested in what the child has to say and praise the child for responding.

- **Types of questions**. Though most foster care professionals are not the ones conducting these interviews, it is helpful to know what types of questions are asked. Protocols vary in different states, counties, and cities. The interviewer is supposed to develop rapport with the child (for example, "What do you like to watch on TV?" "Do you like pizza?") and make a quick assessment of the developmental level so the interviewer knows how to pitch the questions. Generally, interviewers avoid open-ended questions like, "Tell me what happened." They use direct questions that focus on the environment, person, and body parts; multiple-choice questions; or yes-no questions. (If you have an interest in learning more about the interview process, Kuehnle [1996] has a nice chapter on this topic.)

A good interviewer knows that preschoolers are illogical, so he or she should avoid asking them "why" questions. A good interviewer also knows that kids do not like to admit that they do not know an answer

and will make something up to respond.
- **Sociocultural issues**. Certain ethnic groups are more comfortable talking to a strange interviewer than others are. Interviewers of the same ethnicity as the client are not always available. In a culture where respect for adults is emphasized, a child may not want to testify against or turn in an adult who abused them. Be aware of cultural values about issues such as shame (many cultures believe shame stays in the family) and the importance of virginity (in a culture where virginity is culturally valued, families may seem unconcerned about abuse that does not involve penetration) [Garcia de la Rocha 1989]. Cultural perspectives regarding homosexuality need to be considered in cases where a same-sex perpetrator molested the child.

Now that we have reviewed aspects that contribute to the accuracy of children's reports, let's consider why some children seem more adversely affected than others.

What Contributes to the Psychological Damage?

Veltkamp and Miller [1994] have a nice section on assessment of the severity or degree of psychological harm, which I have summarized here with accompanying comments about foster care.
- **Age of the child**. If the child was young enough not to know what was happening, damage is lessened. Generally, the older the child and more capable of understanding what was happening, the greater the impairment. Young children who have been abused or exposed to a highly sexualized environment can initially present severe symptoms, but they tend to respond more readily to treatment than the older children. If the child is under 18 months of age and abuse was not painful, the child would not understand it was wrong, would not disclose because he/she does not understand the meaning of it, and would be minimally affected. School-aged children know sexual behavior is wrong and are likely to believe that they are "bad" for participating in the behavior—even if they were coerced or forced. Adolescents fully understand the concept of exploitation and consequences of illicit sex acts.

  To summarize, *older child = more trauma.*
- **Duration**. The longer and the more times the abuse has occurred, the greater the psychological disturbance.

  Longer duration = more trauma.

- **Aggression**. Many children in foster care survive multiple abuses including sexual and physical abuse, psychological abuse, and neglect. It is not unusual for child victims of concurrent physical and sexual abuse to describe the physical abuse as more traumatic.

  More aggression with sexual abuse = more trauma.

- **Threats**. The presence or absence of threats to the child or the child's loved ones has an effect on the severity of the abuse. One foster child denied sexual abuse for a significant period of time despite consensus by team members that she had been abused. The child made a disclosure after her father died; the father was the perpetrator and had threatened both the child and the birth mother with a gun, saying he would kill them both if they disclosed the abuse. The birth mother never told, although the abuse had gone on for years with her knowledge. If the child and the mother had not been threatened with bodily harm, one or more of them might have disclosed the abuse years earlier, thus preventing extreme acting out in the child, which resulted in both residential and foster placement.

  The greater the threat = more trauma.

- **Relationship with perpetrator**. For many victims, it is psychologically easier if the perpetrator is a stranger. The closer the child's relationship with the person, the harder it is for the child to make sense of it. The child's perspective is, "Why would someone who cares about me hurt me?" Developmentally it is easier for a child to comprehend a "bad man" who is a stranger hurting them than someone they felt close to and considered to be a "good man."

  More intimacy = more trauma.

- **Degree of activity**. The more types of abuse and more physical contact, the more traumatic it is for the child. One child was abused for a period of years by a brother's friend who slept over at the home a lot. The boy went everywhere with the family and was like another son. He also turned out to be abusing all of the girls in the family over a long period of time. After the disclosure, it took the girls about a year in therapy to start addressing the abuse.

  More often abused = more trauma.

- **Whether significant adults believe disclosure**. Support by adults who are close to the child is a significant factor in sexual abuse. When a child is in foster care, he or she may disclose previous or ongoing sexual abuse to the foster parent, social worker, therapist, or other team member. Because foster children display copious clinical problems, including lying and stealing, it is tempting to dismiss an abuse allegation as yet another lie or manipulation. When the abuse allegations are true and the adult who was told does not believe the child, the psychological ill effects can be devastating. The child becomes increasingly distrustful and feels he or she has no one to turn to. Because of these possibilities, it is important to rely on professionals skilled in interviewing for sexual abuse, no matter what our instincts are as parents or mental health professionals. We should never take the chance that the child is not lying, because we cannot protect that child without a thorough investigation.

More disbelief = more trauma

Training Exercise: Child's Interpretation of Abuse

Kuehnle [1996] has a great chart that illustrates the relationship between Piaget's stages of cognitive development and the child's interpretation of sexual abuse. She has a similar chart relating the effects of abuse to moral development. These would make good overheads for discussion with foster parents or mental health staff.

Interviewing the Child

We have already discussed some aspects of interviewing the child. If you would like to read more about the difference between clinical and forensic interviews, see Kuehnle [1996]. Generally, a child is interviewed by an employee of a social welfare agency who is a social worker or other mental health professional. Interviewers like to see the child alone so that adults will not influence what the child says, but there are inherent problems with the interview of an abused child alone in a room with a stranger. A good interviewer will acknowledge the child's possible discomfort and explain why people who care about the child would ask him or her to answer the questions of a stranger.

Kuehnle[1996] describes four kinds of questions: (1) Open-ended questions, which are most useful with very young children but are less likely to result in detailed descriptions of the abuse event(s); (2) Directive questions, which can be either focused on persons, places, or body parts ("What does Mr. M do that you don't like?") or can be multiple choice ("Were you in Mr. M's house, your house, or at school when this happened?"); (3) Yes-No questions, which are considered too leading by some professionals because children may pick the response they perceive the interviewer wants to hear. On the other hand, we need children to be clear about whether abuse occurred or not, and this requires a yes-no response; (4) Coercive questions, which are not acceptable because they make it clear what answer the interviewer expects to hear ("He touched your penis, didn't he?").

In most child welfare settings, there is a specific set of questions interviewers will ask. A member of the treatment team could request a list of these questions or obtain them for use in foster parent training. Children should not be asked questions by foster parents or others on the treatment team. Research shows that the more times children are interviewed, the more the story changes. Also, the interview information may be needed as court testimony.

Sometimes agencies set up interview appointments for siblings at the same location, one after another. If it is the case that one sibling was molested by another, this scenario reduces the chances that the victim will tell on the perpetrator, if only because they make eye contact in the waiting room. Two brothers, 3 and 5 years of age, were scheduled to be interviewed by an investigator at the same time as their 13-year-old sister, who was one of the people who had molested them. Even though the sister was in a juvenile detention facility for other offenses, the agency arranged all the interviews back-to-back. The boys would talk to their therapists about how the sister sexually and physically abused them, but would not say a word to the investigator. All it took was one look from the 13-year-old sister to silence both boys.

Also be aware that appointments may be set up for a 3- or 4-year-old at nap time, or for an older child when he or she is missing an important school or family activity. Team members need to be assertive in requesting a better appointment time that could maximize the chances of the child speaking with the investigator. A child who is missing a birthday party is less likely to cooperate and give a reliable report. It is also undesirable for foster children to miss school to be interviewed, since many of them missed some school during the placement process and have educational problems that can best be addressed by consistent school attendance. Finally, some investigators interview children in the school building, both for convenience and the perception that this is a comfortable, yet neutral location for an interview. Team members need to consider the feasibility of such a plan based on the individual case.

Children sometimes deny that abuse occurred after they have made a disclosure. This is called recanting and there is a lot of research on this subject. Studies have shown that in many cases of documented sexual abuse, most children deny it the first time they are asked [Sorensen & Snow 1991].

If the foster parents cannot prepare the child for the interview, what can they do? They should avoid telling the child about the interview too far in advance. How far in advance is often best judged by the foster parents if they have known the child for a period of time. Keep home routines the same. Provide emotional support as it seems appropriate for the individual child. When the child completes the interview, praise him/her for doing his/her best, even if the child did not talk. Avoid saying things like, "Why didn't you talk to that lady?" which will only increase the child's anxiety about telling at some time in the future.

Assessment Tools

Interviewing the child is only one way of learning about the child's abuse experiences. Psychologists and social workers have developed instruments that can help treatment teams to learn more about sexualized behavior. Though child interviewing is probably the most common technique used with foster care youth, there are many useful assessment tools that provide clinical information for treatment of children who have been sexually abused.

Standardized Behavior Problem Rating Scales

Standardized behavior problem rating scales can be administered to foster parents and teachers. For these, the parent or foster parent fills out a questionnaire about a variety of behaviors, including sexual behaviors. Many agencies use these program-wide for outcome research or quality improvement (e.g., to document effectiveness of the programs). Usually these rating scales contain a handful of items on sexualized behavior. These questionnaires will not identify abused versus nonabused children consistently, but can give valuable information for treatment teams. For a highly technical discussion of the statistical properties of these scales with regard to sexual abuse, refer to Kuehnle [1996]. Some of the popular and well-researched scales used nationwide include:
- **Child Behavior Checklist** [Achenbach 1991, 1992]. This is designed to record the behavioral problems and competencies of children aged 2 through 16, as reported by parents or other caregivers.

Anatomical Dolls

For years we used anatomical dolls as a part of standardized sexual abuse interviews. Anatomical dolls are special dolls sold to mental health professionals, mainly through catalogs. The dolls are usually made of cloth, look to be handmade, and have detailed genitalia. For example, pubic hair on adult dolls is made of yarn or embroidered on the cloth. Typically, the dolls have easily removable clothing. Years ago, it was thought that if children played with the dolls in sexualized ways, it was evidence that abuse occurred. Dolls were used because young children have limited language ability. In a sense, the play takes the place of words. After years of operating under the assumption that sexual play with the dolls meant sexual abuse, researchers found out this was not true.

Research has shown that the dolls might increase children's suggestibility to report abuse when none occurred, and therefore they are now seen in a limited way as a diagnostic tool (see Goodman & Aman [1990] for a review). Also, nonabused children may explore the dolls' body parts, which could mistakenly be interpreted as a reenactment of past abuse. In some research, the sexually victimized children actually avoid the dolls more than the nonabused controls. The current thinking about ways the dolls can be useful is summarized below:

- As an icebreaker to show body parts.
- As an anatomical model. Anatomical dolls can be used to determine child's sexual knowledge and understanding of body functions.
- As a demonstration aid: "Show me what happened with..."
- As a memory stimulus. The dolls might trigger the child's memory of what happened.

- **Conners Rating Scales** [Conners 1990]. This behavior rating system, composed of two scales—the Teacher Rating Scales and the Conners' parent rating scale—is useful in identifying hyperactivity and other behavioral problems.

- **Personality Inventory for Children, Revised Format** [Wirt 1990]. This inventory, which consists of 420 true or false questions, provides comprehensive and clinically relevant descriptions of child behavior, affect, and cognitive status, as well as family characteristics.

- **Devereux Scales of Mental Disorders** [Naglieri et al. 1994]. The Devereux Scales were developed to aid in the identification of behaviors associated with psychopathology and cover areas related to conduct, attention, anxiety, depression, autism, and other acute problems in children ages 6 to 18.

Standard Child Abuse Rating Scales

Instruments designed to measure specific sexual behaviors have been developed. Both of the instruments listed below have been developed by experts in the field of child sexual abuse and have been researched for several years. These measures are not yet widely used in foster care, but could be valuable tools in assessment of sexually abused children. Several instruments that are appropriate for use with adolescents can be found in Kruczek & Vitanza [1999], but they have not been as widely researched as the two mentioned above.

- **Child Sexual Behavior Inventory (CSBI-R)** [Friedrich et al. 1992]. This 35-item parent report assesses sexual behavior related to self-stimulation, sexual aggression, gender-role behavior, and personal boundary violations in children ages 2 to 12.
- **Child Sexual Behavior Checklist** (2nd ed.) [Johnson 1996]. This instrument was developed to measure sexual behavior problems in children under the age of 12. The first part asks questions about behaviors relating to sex and sexuality. Subsequent sections ask about social circumstances that could contribute to sexual acting out and asks the respondents to describe sexual behaviors of concern.

Rating Scales for Posttraumatic Stress

Because many abused children show symptoms of PTSD, these scales could be useful in foster care. Though not yet widely used in the foster care setting, these instruments could provide valuable information for assessment and treatment.

- **Child Dissociative Checklist**. This 20-item checklist asks the parent to rate the extent to which 20 symptoms relating to dissociation in children ages 6 to 12 years, including dissociative amnesia, rapid shifts in behavior, trance-like states, hallucinations, identity changes, and aggressive and sexual behaviors.
- **Children's Impact of Traumatic Events Scale-Revised** [Wolfe et al. 1987]. This 54-item self-report scale is administered by an interviewer. It examines issues of betrayal, guilt, helplessness, intrusive thoughts, sexualization, and stigmatization in the trauma survivor.

- **Trauma Symptom Checklist** [Briere 1989]. This assessment instrument, which consists of 54 items, measures the long-term psychological impacts of childhood sexual abuse in children 8 to 18 years of age. The areas covered include anxiety, depression, dissociation, posttraumatic symptoms, anger, and sexual problems.

- **PTSD Reaction Index** [Pynoos et al. 1987]. This is another self-report interview measure, which focuses on the extent to which the child is affected by flashbacks and reliving the trauma. There is a corresponding parent form where parents comment on PTSD symptoms.

Psychological Testing

Psychological tests are useful in many ways, but were not designed to discriminate between abused and nonabused children. There is insufficient research regarding their use in this manner. However, psychological testing is good to have for a comprehensive clinical picture of the child. Often psychological assessment with children employs assessment of artwork. These techniques, however, are not standardized, nor have they been researched adequately as assessment tools for use with sexually abused children.

- **Thematic Apperception Test** [Bellak 1993]. A test administered by a trained psychologist where the child is shown vague pictures and asked to tell a story about each one. The responses are evaluated with respect to the main theme, main hero, needs and drives of the hero, and how the story depicts the child's view of interpersonal relationships, primary conflicts, and worries and consequences for transgressions.

- **Rorschach** [Exner 1986]. Another test administered by a trained psychologist, the Rorschach involves showing 10 inkblots to the child who responds by describing what he or she sees. The ambiguity of the blots allows the respondent to impose his or her own thoughts, views of interpersonal relationships, concerns, problem-solving style, and coping mechanisms on the stimulus.

- **House-Tree-Person** [Buck 1970]. This is one version of the use of standardized child drawings in psychological assessment. In this test, the child is asked to draw a house, a tree, and a person. Drawings are scored using specific criteria revealing the developmental maturity of the child.

Medical Examinations

Medical examination may be required in some sexual abuse cases. Usually children are taken to see a team of nurses and physicians who specialize in sexual abuse recovery. These treatment teams are often based in university hospitals or teaching hospitals. Sometimes children are sedated for the examination if it is felt that the genital examination will traumatize the child further. The physicians check the appearance of the genitalia and look for abnormalities, like scar tissue from tearing. They measure the genital openings and compare the measurements to norms for children of the corresponding age/size. It is important for the foster parents and/or birth parents to be present for the assessment to provide support for the child.

The best way to support a child before and during the examination is to treat it like any other medical appointment. Tell the child what to expect in words he or she can understand. Here are some examples:

- **Preschooler:** "We need to go see a special doctor today who checks private parts (or use the name of genitalia the child recognizes). It may tickle a bit, but we need to be sure that your private parts are healthy. I'll stay with you while the doctor checks you. When you are done, we'll have a treat."

- **School-aged:** "Today we are going to see a special doctor who checks private parts. Because [Name of Perpetrator] was touching your private parts, we want to be sure everything is all right with those parts. The doctor will check you in a new way that you have not been checked before; you may feel a little embarrassed that the doctor is spending so much time checking your parts. I can stay with you in the room if you like. It will take about [how many] minutes. When we are done, the doctor will tell you what she found out. When you are done, we'll also have a treat. Do you have any questions?"

- **Teenager:** Same as school-aged, but modify as follows, "The doctor needs to measure your genital openings and compare her measurements to what is normal for kids your age. She will be looking for evidence of sexual abuse, which can help to make it so that [Name of Perpetrator] cannot molest other kids. She will also do a pregnancy test (if a girl) and check for sexually transmitted diseases. It can be really hard to have the doctor/nurse looking at your private parts, but this is what they need to do to be sure you are healthy. Would you like to do something afterward to reward you for your hard work?"

Foster parents could call the clinic to find out the name of the physician, gender, and description of the physician. It helps kids to know what to expect (e.g., he's a tall, white man with a soft voice). They could find out if there will be a nurse present or anyone else in the room, and ask whether the examining room will look any different to a child than a typical pediatrician visit. They can get details about how long it will take, whether they will have to wait, and what the child will be told by the staff. If the foster parent does not wish to gather this information, it is appropriate for another team member, like the social worker or therapist, to get the information to share with the foster parent and child. This preparation will decrease the anxiety of both the child and the foster parent.

Unless the foster parent is philosophically opposed, providing the child with some kind of treat or positive reinforcement is a good idea. The child should be positively reinforced whether or not the child cooperates. Though child abuse medical specialists and their staff tend to be exceptionally sensitive to how difficult the exams can be for children, many foster parents view it as just another routine medical appointment. It is not routine and requires higher levels of support than a physical or teeth cleaning.

If the child wants to talk about what happened, foster parents can use their best judgment in doing so. If the child does not want to talk about it, foster parents should acknowledge their cooperation or how difficult it was for the child (if this is true) and leave it at that. The child should not be interrogated about the exam if the clinic prefers that the foster parents not be present.

A written report will be submitted to the agency requesting the medical assessment. Foster parents may or may not be told results after the assessment, depending on legal aspects of the case. Find out ahead of time whether the foster parent will get feedback.

False Allegations

All allegations of sexual abuse require a sexual abuse assessment. A large body of research looks at how to tell if a child is telling the truth or making a false report in the assessment process. There is little written about the topic of false allegations with respect to foster care. Why do children make false allegations against their foster parents? Foster parents may feel that a child who is already acting out may be intentionally making false allegations to be mean to the foster parent or foster family.

On the contrary, experts say that kids may make false allegations because they are reenacting the abuse (the "flashbacks" mentioned earlier in the description of posttraumatic stress disorder). Another possibility is that the child may be confusing fantasy with reality because the child has lost his/her grasp of reality as a result of trauma and instability.

Sometimes children do make up the allegations because they are feeling close to the foster family, and this closeness is unfamiliar or scary. They make the allegations to get away from the foster family because they fear if they get close, then the foster family will reject or hurt them too. Unfortunately, many false allegations result in the child being moved to a different foster home. Ironically, this is the last thing she or he needs, whether the allegations are made for any of the reasons above. If the child is traumatized and confused, the child needs the stability of the home he has known since he was taken from his other stable, though chaotic environment. If the child fears attachment, she needs to learn that if she gets close to the family, they will not hurt or leave her.

One good way to protect foster parents is to establish good working relationships on the treatment team. It is also important to facilitate the foster child having good relationships with key adults so that in the unlikely event a problem arises, you all are accustomed to working closely together. In short, good teaming is essential.

Whenever a child makes a child abuse allegation, it has to be taken seriously, even if team members think the child is lying to get out of trouble or to retaliate for something someone in the family did. In most states, it is also against the law not to report allegations of abuse, even if they appear to be unsubstantiated. Being calm, going through the appropriate professional channels, and not panicking are essential here. If the child is lying, he/she will see that adults are going to be calm, listen to her, and weigh the evidence in a careful manner. Often if kids are lying and the matter is approached without hysteria, they admit to a false report.

The other reason to take them seriously is that sometimes kids are sexually traumatized in foster care. Sometimes the foster family has a friend or family member with a problem that no one has known or talked about. None of us like to admit that we have people with serious problems, like sexual problems, in our families. But some of us do. In one case, an elderly, senile grandfather in the foster home was making sexual overtures to a promiscuous, acting-out teenager. The foster family maintained that the teenager was lying. There was evidence, however, that suggested this man was indeed highly inappropriate in his behavior.

The other thing that happens is that a family member has not been made aware of how to behave around sexually abused youth and may be doing something that is overstimulating, which leads to some kind of sexual encounter. One example might be a teenage girl who lives in a home where the foster parents have an adult son who does not live with them. Suppose the son is visiting and is sleeping on the hide-a-bed in the living room and neglects to consider that sleeping in boxer shorts/briefs may be too overstimulating for a teenage girl. Maybe this teenager is already a little worked up about this young man. One thing leads to another, and there may be consensual (but illicit) sexual activity.

Now, foster parents cannot broadcast to every member of the family that the child is abused and dictate how they act, but they can and should take steps to keep sexual behavior or appearance to a minimum. For example, foster parents of a sexually reactive teenager boy can tell an adult daughter who is visiting to keep her coat on if she is dressed in a sexy outfit for date. Adult children may need to be asked to watch how they act with spouses or significant others while visiting the foster home. One abused child reported thinking about her own sexual abuse when she saw the foster mother's adult daughter sit on her boyfriend's lap while the daughter and the boyfriend were watching the kids. Several weeks later, this child was caught with her younger brother on her lap, playing in an obviously sexualized way.

The other thing that is likely to decrease the chances of false allegations is to have the proper structure in the home so foster parents know who is where, and when. Foster parents need not be detectives. But if they run a tight ship, so to speak, they will know what is going on in their home. This means that if there are a bunch of kids playing in the basement or talking, the foster parent cruises by once in a while.

Now that we have covered the subject of identifying the sexually abused child in foster care, the next question is what to do for the child to help him or her heal.

TABLE 3.1

The Relationship Between Piaget's Stages of Cognitive Development* and the Child's Interpretations of Sexual Abuse

Development Stage	General Age Range	Characteristics of Piaget's Stages	Child's Interpretations of Sexual Abuse
Sensorimotor	Birth to approximately 18 months	• Preverbal • Child begins to construct basic concepts of objects • Development of the concept of object permanence (approximately 8 or 9 months) • Play primarily involves imitation and copying the actions of others without understanding the purpose of the actions • Self-concept is limited to a physical awareness that one has a body	• Child, if engaged in sex play that was not painful, would not understand it was wrong • Child unlikely to verbally disclose sexual exploitation because does not understand the meaning of it • Sexually abused child would not identify himself/herself as "bad" or "dirty" • Child does not understand "intention" – so would not identify the perpetrator as "bad" if told the sexual behavior was "good"
Preoperational	18 months to approximately 7 to 8 years	• Beginning of organized language and symbolic thought • Child begins to perceive language as a tool to get needs met • Much of child's language is egocentric – he or she talks to self and does not listen to other children • Child does not use logical thinking. As a result, cannot reason by implication • Child's reasoning is transductive reasoning: reasoning from a particular idea to a particular idea without logically connecting them	• Child does not understand "intention" – so would not identify the perpetrator as "bad" • Child can be easily manipulated through curiosity or fear. Child will believe the perpetrator has supernatural powers if given this information by the perpetrator (i.e., if told by the perpetrator he or she at all times will know what the child tells others, child will accept this information as valid) • A child who tells a preposterous story of sexual abuse, whether the story be fabricated out of repeated questioning or an embellishment of an actual experience, will have little awareness of the illogical nature of the story
Concrete Operations	7 to 8 years to 11 to 12 years	• Thinking is concrete rather than abstract • Child can now perform and make basic groupings of classes and relations • Child can now see how consequences follow from action – reasoning ability enables the child to acquire and follow directions	• Child understands sexual behavior is wrong, child may believe he/she is bad because he/she is engaged in "bad" behavior • A child who is sexually abused can be manipulated into worrying about the consequences to the perpetrator without having insight into consequences for himself or herself
Formal Operations	11 to 12 years to 14 to 15 years	• Formal (abstract) thought marked by the appearance of hypothetical deductive reasoning • Child can now arrange various ideas in various ways	• Child who is sexually abused may now begin to understand the concept of exploitation and think about the consequences to himself or herself of the sexual abuse • Child who is not sexually abused may be capable of independently initiating a false allegation for reasons of attention, of revenge, or to escape an emotionally/physically abusive family

* The Stages of Cognitive Developement were adapted from *Carmichael's Manual of Child Psychology* (Vol. 1, 3rd ed., pp. 703-730), by P. Mussen (Ed.), 1970, chapter entitled "Piaget's Theory" by J. Piaget, New York: John Wiley & Sons, Copyright © 1970 by John Wiley & Sons, Inc. Reprinted by permission of John Wiley & Sons, Inc. Also from *Piaget's Theory of Intellectual Development*, by H. Ginsburg and S. Opper, 1969, Englewood Cliffs, NJ: Prentice-Hall. The child's interpretations of sexual abuse were formulated by the author.

TABLE 3.2

The Relationship Between Kohlberg's Stages of Moral Development* and the Child's Interpretations of Sexual Abuse

Development Stage	Characteristics of Kohlberg's Stages	Child's Interpretations of Sexual Abuse
Preconventional Morality (ages 4 to 10) Rules and social expectations are something internal to the self Emphasis is on external control – Motivation to conform to external rules is related to avoidance of punishment or acquiring rewards	Stage 1 (4 yrs to 8 yrs): • Individual's definition of right or wrong is based on obedience to rules and authority • Individual's motivation to conform to external rules is based on avoidance of punishment or on obtaining rewards • Confusion of authority's perspective with one's own Stage 2 (8 yrs to 10 yrs): • Individual conforms to the rules out of self-interest and assessment of what others can do for him or her • Individual's motivation to conform to external rules is based on the desire to collect rewards for conformity	• In the beginning of this stage, the sexually abused child may readily conform to the instructions of adults without understanding that the sexual behavior is wrong • Child can be tricked into believing their sexual involvement is special, fun, or normal • Child most likely will not intentionally verbally disclose the abuse because of obedience to authority • Child is vulnerable to do what others tell him or her to do, including following directions to lie that sexual abuse did not happen or to lie that sexual abuse did happen • Sexually abused child may understand wrongfulness of sexual exploitation but conforms to the instructions of adults to please adults or to avoid punishment • If relationship with perpetrator is child's strongest relationship, child most likely will not disclose. If child's relationship with nonoffending parent is supportive, likelihood of disclosure is greater • Child continues to be vulnerable to do what others tell him or her, including lying about the absence or presence of their involvement in sexual abuse
Conventional Morality of Role Conformity (ages 10 to 13) Rules and expectations of others, especially authority figures, have been internalized by the self Emphasis is on being considered good by those persons whose opinions are important – Children have internalized the standards of others to some extent	Stage 3 (10 yrs to 12 yrs): • Control of behavior is externally derived – the standards are set by rules and expectations held by individuals who are identified as authority • The individual's motivation is to gain approval and to please others • Reactions of authority serve as cues to the rightness or wrongness of an act • Motivation becomes internal as the child anticipates the praise or censure of significant others Stage 4 (12 yrs to 13 yrs): • Individual's motivation to conform to external rules is based on maintaining social order and showing respect for authority • Individual is able to take the perspective of others	• Sexually abused child understands the wrongfulness of the sexual exploitation and may disclose the abuse • If supportive relationships exist within the home or outside of the home, apart from the perpetrator, and these relationships become more significant than relationship with the perpetrator, child may disclose (to a friend, teacher, etc.) • Child who is not having emotional needs met by caregivers could make a false allegation of abuse in order to gain nurturance from others • Sexually abused child understands the wrongfulness of the sexual exploitation and understands the consequences to the perpetrator if sexual abuse is disclosed

| Postconventional Morality or Principled Morality (earliest development age 13; some people never develop)

Rules and expectations of other are differentiated from self, and values are defined in terms of independently chosen principles

This level is the attainment of true morality - the individual understands the possibility of conflict between two socially accepted standards and tries to decide between them | Stage 5 (early adolescent and up):
• Individual's motivation to conform to external rules is based on defining right and wrong in terms of laws. These laws and rules are seen as necessary for institutional functioning
• Considers moral and legal points of view; recognizes that they sometimes conflict | • Sexually abused child understands the wrongfulness of the sexual exploitation and may disclose so perpetrator will not hurt others |
| | Stage 6 (middle to late adolescence and up);
• A belief in the validity of universal moral principles and a sense of personal commitment to them
• Individual does what he or she thinks is right, regardless of the legal restrictions or opinions of others | • Sexually abused child assesses the sexual exploitation and does what he or she thinks is right |

* The Stages of Moral Development adapted from *Moral Development and Behavior: Theory, Research and Social Issues* (pp. 31-53), by T. Lickona (Ed.), chapter entitled "Moral Stage and Moralization: The Cognitive Developmental Approach" by L. Kohlberg, 1976. New York: Holt, Rinehart & Winston. Reprinted with permission. The child's interpretations of sexual abuse were formulated by the author.

5

Treatment of Sexual Abuse

Before I begin the discussion of what treatment could or should consist of, I first want to look at some of its limitations and clear up some common misconceptions that foster parents might have.

Misconceptions about Therapy

A common misconception about sexual abuse treatment is that it is good to talk about the sexual trauma. As adults, somehow we assume that it is always better for children to talk about a problem. With emotional trauma, this is not always the case, and this can be true for both children and adults. Sometimes a child needs a long time before he or she can talk about what happened. Treatment team members need to respect that and to be careful not to push the child to do something he or she is not ready for. One of the reasons talking is not always helpful is that sometimes talking about the trauma in the wrong way or at the wrong time can retraumatize the child. How can you tell? Usually if it is too much too soon, there is regression in the child's behavior. This means the child goes back to doing old problem behaviors she had stopped doing or she acts like a younger child in some ways.

Some regression during treatment is normal and should be expected. Many children who start therapy for sexual abuse and other concerns start to act out more in the foster home. The foster parents immediately get upset with the therapist, who they see as provoking problem behaviors. Again, a close alliance between foster parents and therapist is essential to managing regression relating to therapy and determining whether too much is being asked of the child. For example, they could have information from the protective services worker that the child may have been abused by uncles. The therapist would try playing out the scenario in the dollhouse, then asking the child directly. If the child then says he doesn't want to talk about it, the therapist might say, "It's okay if you're not ready to talk about it today. I'd like to ask you about your uncles some other time."

Another misconception foster parents have about therapy is that the therapist will find out how the child is abused, and this will help to solve the problems. In many cases, it is impossible to determine exactly how much and in what ways the child was abused or by whom. If you recall the earlier section on interviewing, most young children cannot reliably provide details about their abuse when they are abused before language skills are developed. The good news is that we can treat childhood sexual abuse without knowing these details. Treatment involves helping children to change their thinking about sexuality, which often has become age-inappropriate, and to help them recognize ways to keep themselves safe.

One last pitfall is for foster parents to see the child abuser as an evil, terrible person who did painful things. Though child abuse is a horrible reality for children, many children had a positive relationship with the perpetrator and continue to have some positive feelings toward that abuser. Some abusers give children food and candy in exchange for sex, which may not be perceived as bothersome by a child in poverty who may not get enough to eat. Also, the sexual things the perpetrator did may have been pleasurable—not painful—to the child. A good approach is something like, "[Name of the Perpetrator] made a mistake touching you like that. Grown-ups are not supposed to touch you like that/play those kinds of games." Children understand about mistakes, and this approach avoids comment about the abuser.

Teamwork

In the assessment phase, I emphasized the importance of teamwork, reasoning that shared information gives a more complete view of the child's experiences. When it comes to the treatment of sexual abuse, teamwork is equally important.

The most important thing to remember about the treatment of sexual abuse in foster children is that treatment does not occur without the involvement of the foster family. Many different types of therapy are used to treat sexual abuse and they will be described below. Even when the child is being seen in individual therapy or group therapy, however, it is important to have close communication and teaming with the foster parents. Many mental health practitioners have taken the approach of seeing the child in a sort of vacuum, an approach where the child is transported to the therapy setting to be "fixed," so to speak. In addition to alienating the foster parents who are team members, this approach teaches the child that therapy has nothing to do with the family he or she lives in.

Children in foster care exhibit a wide array of sexualized behaviors in the foster home. Therapy needs to include the individuals who observe and are affected by these behaviors—the foster parents. This way, the therapist can team with foster parents to share strategies for coping with sexualized behaviors in the home. Finally, the therapist will learn important information about the child's adjustment through a good relationship with the foster family, which will facilitate the therapy.

The following is a list of what each team member brings to treatment of the sexually abused child:

- **Foster parents**. They usually know the child the best because they take care of the child 24 hours a day, 7 days a week. They have the closest emotional bond with the child, with the exception of the birth family in some, but not all cases. They have a wealth of information on the child's functioning in various areas.

- **Social worker**. Some children have two social workers, one for the county or other locale that holds the custody of the child. The role of the agency social worker is to monitor the "big picture" to ensure that the child gets the services he or she needs. Different agencies vary with respect to how much involvement there is in treatment. All treatment does need to be approved by the person in this role, however.

- **Case manager/social worker/home visitor**. In different agencies there are different titles referring to the person who visits the home to support the foster family and monitor the day-to-day needs of the child. Usually these professionals are social workers, but they may also have other educational training. Sometimes these individuals are also the therapist for the child, and indeed may have the title "therapist." They are trained in sexual abuse assessment and treatment. Their role is to be more attuned to the day-to-day adjustment of the foster child and to give and receive input to the foster parents.

- **Therapist/counselor**. The role of the therapist in treatment is to provide the actual therapy, including individual, group, or family psychotherapy. They need to team with others to get the information they need to do the therapy. Their job is also to give information back to the team on social and developmental issues addressed in therapy. The therapist is knowledgeable in the research and clinical knowledge about sexual abuse treatment. The therapist, by virtue of training, should have a unique view of the child's social and emotional functioning.

- **Psychologist**. Not all teams have a psychologist, but if they do, the role of the psychologist may be to administer and/or interpret psychological test data. Sometimes the psychologist's role is to provide more clinical expertise as a consultant to the team. The psychologist is also knowledgeable about sexual abuse assessment and treatment.

- **Psychiatrist**. The psychiatrist's role is to address issues relating to medication or to provide clinical expertise from a medical framework. Psychiatrists have had extensive training in abuse recovery and trauma. They may also serve as clinical consultants.

- **Birth family**. Not all teams involve birth families, but when they do, the role of the birth family is to learn about treatment provided for the child and to participate in the treatment as indicated. The birth family members may or may not know the child best, depending on history. When there is cooperation, birth family members' knowledge about the child can be invaluable.

- **Child or adolescent**. Not all agencies consider the child a part of the treatment team, but if they do, the role of the child on the team is to participate in treatment and to give feedback on how the treatment is progressing from his/her perspective.

Children Can't Wait

Another key to treatment is knowing when and how to make the child feel comfortable addressing the issues in the context of foster care. This involves a second major rule about treatment of sexual abuse: therapists are trained to develop rapport with children before they try to discuss sexual topics and problems, but often foster parents and case managers do not have the luxury of getting to know a child before addressing these issues. Maybe the child is walking around the house naked the second day of placement, and the family cannot ignore the behavior until they have developed a relationship with the child. A good approach in this case is to say something like, "Penny, I don't know you too well yet because you have only lived here for a few days, but in our house, children need to wear clothes unless they are in the bathroom. A foster parent is someone you can talk to privately about things that have to do with your body. I am wondering if there is some reason you don't feel comfortable with your clothes on." Of course, you would need to adjust what you say to the age of the child. The other thing to remember along these lines is that you want to be a good listener and not be doing all the talking in these situations.

Individual Therapy

Understanding the nuts and bolts of therapy, that is, the kinds of things therapists do with foster children in therapy, is one cornerstone of good teaming. Therapists use different approaches with children of different ages.

Preschoolers

As mentioned above, preschool therapy usually involves the foster parents and, if possible, the birth parents. At this age, the therapist needs to have good play therapy skills and is likely to work a lot with a dollhouse to portray family interactions. The therapist might also use puppets or stuffed animals to address key issues. Some therapeutic work on expressing basic feelings (sad, mad, glad) is also common. Depending on the age of the preschooler, the therapist might use some therapeutic books such as those listed below:

- *A Very Touching Book* by J. Hindman
- *It's My Body* by L. Freeman
- *Red Flag, Green Flag People: A Personal Safety Program for Children* by K. S. Freed
- *Do You Have a Secret?* by P. Russell & B. Stone

School-Aged Children

Therapeutic games and books are used frequently in individual therapy with school-aged children. Though some children are able to talk about their abuse experiences, children are unlikely to discuss feelings and concerns the way adults do. If you do not have a library of therapeutic games and books available to you, children enjoy making books on this topic and playing therapeutic games [Shapiro 1994]. Individual play therapy is also used with school-aged children, employing materials such as the dollhouse, puppets, action figures, or board games. Marvasti [1989] reviews the different approaches to play therapy with sexually abused children and the stages of therapy with illustrative clinical examples. He also describes a variety of play diagnostic and therapy techniques, including mutual storytelling, dream analysis, role reversal, and role-play. Children also respond well in individual therapy to making illustrated books about their abuse and life history.

Adolescents

Talking is generally more successful with adolescents than games or books. Some books can be effective with this age group such as *The Playbook for Kids About Sex,* by J. Blank and M. Quackenbush, and *Sex Stuff for Kids,* by C. S. Marsh (see the resources section). It is also advantageous to use books on normative sexuality for adolescents described in Chapter 2. Another useful technique with adolescents is writing their life story, which can be done using a computer or writing it out longhand, with the therapist serving as the "secretary." Some teenagers enjoy writing abuse-related fiction or poetry. Generally, with adolescents in individual therapy, abuse is one of many issues on the treatment plan. In foster care, the sexually abused adolescent may be a youth who has been in long-term foster care, who has been in several foster homes, and who is looking toward independent living. Sexual abuse treatment occurs in the context of discussions about dating, peer relations, and family rules.

Group Therapy

Child and adolescent groups are widely used in the treatment of sexual abuse. These groups tend to include structured activities that both educate and provide opportunities for expression of feelings. In foster care, one of the impediments to group treatment is having enough children of the same age to run a group and at the time that all the children need the group. Group treatment is often the treatment of choice, because children who have been through a similar abuse experience can understand

---

**Training Exercise:
Treating Sexual Abuse in the Foster Home**

Read some of the sexual abuse books used for kids aloud and explore how they might be used in the foster home.

the child differently than adults. Group therapy is also cost effective for agencies that must serve many children and adolescents on a limited agency budget. In adolescence, group therapy is particularly important because teenagers normally turn to other youth for support and validation. For children of all ages, the group experience helps to foster feelings of normalcy and reduces feelings of stigmatization [Berliner & Ernst 1984].

Preschoolers

Preschool groups can be held while the parents have a parent support group. Preschool sexual abuse groups typically involve a "getting to know you" activity to aid the young child in making the transition to a structured session. There is frank but age-appropriate discussion about why the children are in group (using terms like "touching problems"). There are simple group rules like keeping hands to oneself and taking turns speaking. The therapists work on basic feelings such as mad, sad, happy, or scared; read books on sexual abuse, such as those mentioned earlier under the section on individual therapy; and plan educational activities on safety. Therapeutic drawing is also used. Stickers are useful as positive reinforcement. These groups tend to be shorter than for older children, lasting maybe 30 minutes in length and meeting for 6 to 8 sessions.

It is important to share the entire curriculum with the parents and to give handouts so the parents can reinforce the material at home. Some groups have the parents join at the end to go over the material for the day.

School-Aged Children

There are many good articles on sexual abuse groups for school-aged (often called latency-aged) children, including Reeker and Ensing [1998], and Berliner and Ernst [1984]. Groups usually last 10 to 12 weeks, are composed of same-sex children (though Reeker and Ensing [1998] describe successful mixed-sex groups), and are highly structured. The following issues are usually covered:

- **Education**. Discussion of group rules, rules about confidentiality, and definition of sexual abuse.

- **Disclosure opportunities**. Typical tasks include writing a letter to the perpetrator about the child's feelings on being abused. Therapists might read stories, poems, or sing songs about abuse, then allow opportunities for disclosure. They may draw pictures about feelings of abuse to elicit disclosure.

- **Feelings**. Various activities designed to increase verbal expression of feelings may be used, including feelings games and commercially available materials on feelings (like the *Talking, Feeling, Doing Game* by R. A. Gardner listed in Resources). Reeker and Ensing [1998] have a good discussion of what makes it difficult to talk about sexual abuse, feelings others had about the child's telling, and feelings about the perpetrator.

- **Cognitive**. Cognitive therapy techniques, designed to help children to change erroneous thinking, are used to alleviate guilt and incorrect perceptions. These techniques teach the use of cognitive self-statements that are designed to correct an incorrect perception— like, "It's not my fault I was raped." The therapist may also teach relaxation techniques to decrease anxiety.

- **Personal safety**. Reeker and Ensing [1998] call this "the right to say no/safe and unsafe touches." There are many commercially available books, audiotapes, and videos on personal safety that teach the abused child how to avoid unsafe situations in the future. *My Body Belongs to Me* by Kristin Baird is a book about personal safety. The video "Safety Protection Tips from a Professional Crime Prevention Educator" is designed for 5- to 10-year-olds. Groups might also role-play personal safety scenarios.

- **Self-esteem**. Many good books and pamphlets are available on self-esteem development. You might look at *Don't Feed the Monster on Tuesday* by Moser & Meton, or the video in the Secret Adventure series by Michael Smith called "Shrug: Self-Worth." A self-esteem board game developed by Becky Hidis called "Kids Count Game" is available for grades 2 to 6. One goal of increasing self-esteem relates to body image, so body-tracing activities and other art techniques can also be highly successful in groups to raise children's self-esteem. Also, work on making and keeping friends usually needs to be done.

- **Normative sexuality**. Giving correct information about normative sexuality is a part of most groups. It is important to coordinate the presentation of this information with foster and birth parents, so that it is generally consistent with the philosophy in the family. For young children, issues like the names for private parts are covered. With older children and teens, reproduction and sexual development can be addressed using books and commercially available materials.

- **Termination**. Groups tend to end on a positive note. Therapists look for a celebratory or symbolic ritual that helps children to have closure. It is a common practice to have a party involving food at the close of a group. Children may receive certificates or gifts symbolizing strength.

Adolescent Groups

With adolescent groups, it is especially important to have similar-aged adolescents in group. It's not advisable to place 13-year-olds with 18-year-olds because they do not have similar issues. Adolescents need some structure, but not as much as school-aged children, because they are better equipped developmentally to discuss feelings. Kruczek & Vitanza [1999] have a nice article on group therapy with adolescents, in which they suggest you address the following issues:

- Abuse-related feelings
- Faulty beliefs regarding abuse
- Abuse prevention skills
- Feelings of isolation and stigmatization
   I would also add the following:
- Court testimony
- Effects on family relationships
- Effects on peer relationships
- Self-esteem

The focus of adolescent groups is to increase age-appropriate adaptive behaviors, such as social skills, and to increase coping skills. Topics that tend to be covered are self-nurturance, relaxation techniques, supportive relationships, assertiveness, dating, sexual harassment, and sexuality education. Teenagers with a history of sexual trauma also tend to have other emotional issues, such as depression. Consequently, these groups tend to address many other treatment issues. Adolescent groups can be time-limited or open. Techniques include discussion, role-playing, artwork, viewing TV or videos related to sexual abuse, reading books on the topic, and creative writing.

Foster Family Support Groups

Faller [1988] describes the use of multiple family groups for sexual abuse treatment. Multiple family groups are meetings of more than one family with common concerns. This format encourages families to support one another and to develop supportive relationships within their community. Multiple family groups in foster care programs are relatively rare but could be a powerful intervention. This therapy format is also cost-effective because one or more therapists can provide treatment to multiple families. One drawback of the approach is that the family and victim might share highly personal material with a large number of people. Barth, Yeaton, and Winterfelt [1994] also describe the goals of foster parent psychoeducational groups:

- To increase knowledge about sexual abuse

- To help the foster parents feel more confident about treatment

- To learn strategies that are successful with these children

- To help maintain the placement

- To form a group of well-trained foster parents who could manage highly sexualized children

- To facilitate the development of the foster parents' relationships with one another so they can support one another after the training is completed

Sibling Groups

With increasing numbers of large sibling groups being sexually abused, sometimes it makes sense to do a sibling group following the appropriate age-group model. If the siblings vary tremendously in age, say aged 3 to 15, then a sibling group may not be a good idea.

Family Therapy

Family therapy is typically used in cases where the child lives in the family where the abuse occurred. A child in a foster home, however, may be involved in family therapy with the birth family prior to reunification, as one example. This type of therapy involves discussion of feelings about the abuse and family members taking responsibility for their part in the abuse. Faller [1988] writes about several key goals of family therapy relating to sexual abuse: changing communication patterns in the family, family rules about sex, and family alliances/structure.

Family therapy with the foster family is indicated if the sexual acting out of the child is intense and affects all members of the foster family in a highly negative way. This therapy does not seek to "analyze" the foster

---

Training Exercise: Therapy

Role-play a therapy group. The group leader will need to prepare clinical profiles for the members.

---

family, but rather seeks to improve family communication and rules. One example might be a sexually abused foster child who peeks at other children at night when they are sleeping, making all the children in the family feel unsafe. A frank family discussion with a therapist could provide some ideas for intervention and allow family members to vent their feelings. Another example could be siblings in foster care who are acting out sexually with one another. Family sessions could be used to talk about behaviors, delineate family rules, and clarify consequences for not following the rules.

Medication

There is no medication for the treatment of sexual abuse. Many children who have been abused have had multiple traumas and symptoms that require medication, however. Children may be treated with antidepressants, medications for aggressive acting out, or medicines for attention-deficit/hyperactivity disorder. When the child has had severe trauma, medication can be very helpful. These decisions must be made after psychiatric assessment and with the support of the entire treatment team.

Treatment Follow-Up

Talking about or reenacting sexual abuse can get many children worked up after therapy. For the child to improve, foster parents need to anticipate that there will be some changes in the child's behavior after therapy. A good strategy to prevent trouble in the family is to schedule some low-key time after the child has therapy. If foster parents pick the child up at therapy and take her or him on a series of errands, to a school or family function or any activity requiring good behavior, the child is likely to act out. If it is not possible for the child to be at home—the safest, most secure place for the child—doing something that allows him/her time to relax may result in things going more smoothly in the family. Though foster parents are not advised to pressure children to discuss therapy

---

Training Exercise: Children's Reactions to Therapy

Practice the foster parent-therapist interchange before and after treatment. Group leaders could prepare scripts like "She's been awful this week..."

---

because the child is entitled to confidentiality, making a comment like, "If you want to talk about therapy later, let me know," leaves the door open for discussion.

Another good strategy is to develop a system of communication with the therapist regarding how therapy went. The therapist could speak with the foster parent at the end of the session, or if someone else transports the child, send a note. Some therapists call the foster parent during the session (that is, if the parents work and the child is transported by a different team member) to communicate important concerns or progress. If foster parents are at work during sessions, explore ways the therapist and foster parents can reach one another during a session if necessary. Foster parents and therapist should meet periodically and/or talk frequently by phone to optimize the therapy experience.

If behaviors become severe, it may also mean the therapist needs to change his/her approach or slow things down in the therapy. For example, in one case the therapist was making a book of the child's drawings of birth family members with an accompanying narrative. The child had been sexually abused by the birth mother's male friends and was thought to have been prostituted. Making the book resulted in intolerable increases in the child's sexualized behavior. The foster parent, who had an excellent working relationship with the therapist, said seriously to the therapist, "I think making the book is causing things to get worse at home. Can you back down on it for a while?" After the therapist ascertained that there had been significant deterioration, the therapist agreed with the foster mother that the book was overstimulating.

This was all communicated to the child in age-appropriate words: "Making this book seems to be getting you to think about sex a lot. We're going to put it away for a while." You can see how important good teaming is in such cases. If the foster parent and therapist were not working well together, the therapist may not have taken the foster parent's input, thinking maybe the foster parent was incompetent. The foster parent might not have given the input in a constructive way, or may have scheduled other activities for the child during therapy time so the child would have to miss therapy.

How to Handle Family Visits

An extremely troubling issue for foster parents is sexualized behavior after family visits. They should take some of the same precautions described previously for acting out after therapy, and avoid planning important or tedious activities for the child after a family visit. Social workers can work with foster parents to schedule visits in a way that allows the foster family to do this.

Another thing for foster parents to do is to check with the social worker or whoever is responsible for the visits about what is going on during the visits that could trigger this behavior. Sometimes a sexually inappropriate sibling in another foster home or a cousin with sexual problems is taking the children to the bathroom. Increased supervision during the visit may be indicated. With one family, the three- and five-year-old boys were behaving increasingly sexualized after visits with their birth family. After some investigation, the team learned that the family was undressing an infant sibling during the visits; a sister was alleged to have been molested by one of the family members attending the visits. Older siblings who had been described as molesting these boys were also present at the unsupervised visits. Team members demanded higher levels of supervision at future visits.

How Foster Parents Can Support Therapy

- Work closely with the therapist.
- Make sure the child gets to scheduled appointments.
- Pass along new information as soon as possible.
- Be honest with the therapist and other team members about whether their suggestions are feasible to implement in your home.
- Learn as much as you can about sexual abuse.

How Therapists Can Support Foster Parents

- Treat the foster parent as an equal on the team and a valuable resource.
- Develop a good working relationship with the foster parent(s).
- If you can, do at least one home visit to have a better idea how the family works. It works out nicely to do a home visit as your first contact because you can meet the child for the first time in a familiar environment.
- Be honest and direct with the foster family about concerns. Tell the foster parent what you will discuss with other members of the team so it does not feel like the therapist is "telling on" the foster parents.
- Share articles or book chapters with the foster parents on topics relating to treatment.

6

Sexually Aggressive Children in Foster Care

So far, we have focused on the child who is the victim of sexual abuse from other children or adults. This chapter focuses on the child who is in fact the *victimizer*, the child who molests other children. We used to think that children who were sexually aggressive toward other children had been abused themselves. The behavior was thought to reflect a compulsion to repeat their own sexual trauma, a reflection of self-hate, and many other factors [Gil 1991]. Research has shown that, though some children who are sexually aggressive have been sexual abuse victims, there are many who have no history of sexual abuse [Widom & Ames 1994]. It is likely that these children have suffered other forms of abuse and/or have had antisocial parenting models.

It is difficult for foster parents and mental health professionals to talk about these children who hurt other children. We do not want to believe that children do those things. In foster care, most children are placed in homes where there are other foster children, biological children of the foster parents, grandchildren, or other family members. Some foster parents baby-sit for family members or as a professional occupation, which creates a unique set of concerns. To effectively foster these children, we first need to discuss the clinical characteristics, then move on to treatment strategies in the foster home.

It has taken years for social workers, psychologists, and psychiatrists to develop a clinical picture of the sexually aggressive child, because professionals and parents resisted viewing a young child or adolescent as a sexual perpetrator, a sex offender, or a rapist. The popular misconception is the child who tricks a younger child into pulling down his/her pants in exchange for candy. What we are really talking about is a child who is constantly thinking about sex, planning how to manipulate weaker or younger individuals into gratifying his or her sexual needs, and a child who sees nothing wrong with his or her behavior [Gil 1994]. The first step in understanding and treating these children is admitting that children can act and think in these ways. If adults deny, dismiss, or minimize aggressive sexual behaviors in children, these children can go on to molest more children and to become more entrenched in an unhealthy belief system about sexuality and power.

There are theories about how children come to act this way, with the most popular being that aggression and sexuality are somehow merged and confused as the child develops. Sex and aggression are generally not concepts that go together, nor do they tend to be a focus in childhood. These children use sophisticated power games by picking younger, less cognitively sophisticated, smaller children to gratify their sexual needs [Johnson & Berry 1989]. Sexually aggressive children employ grooming and predatory behaviors, bribery, and coercion to get sex. The sexual behaviors can run the gamut from voyeurism to rape, and can include all of the acts listed in Chapter 3.

Children age 6 to 12 years generally present differently than the adolescent sex offender. Children with sexually aggressive behaviors tend to have behavior problems at home, low self-esteem, immaturity, few outside interests, and often no friends [Gil 1994]. They lack problem-solving skills and demonstrate poor impulse control [Johnson & Berry 1989]. Often, they are physically aggressive as well.

Assessment of Sexually Aggressive Children and Adolescents

Children and adolescents who have been sexually aggressive need to be assessed in a different way than described earlier in Chapter 4. Interviewers who work with these children need special training with this population; these children are good at covering things up and getting adults off track, so examiners need to be armed with special interview techniques and instruments. Exceptional care needs to be taken in reviewing the child's history and in talking with birth family (if available) about the history of sexualized and molesting behaviors.

The interview begins with the interviewer conveying his/her readiness to hear what the child has to say about his/her sexually aggressive behavior. The interviewer tells the child that he/she is aware of the child's "touching problems," and the purpose of the interview is not to punish the child, but to get the child the right kind of help. Confidentiality is discussed; essentially, there is no confidentiality about sexual behaviors

---

Training Exercise: Sexually Abused—or Aggressive?

Here is a good group discussion question: How can you tell the difference between a sexually abused child and one that molests?

---

with respect to team members. One key to treatment is full disclosure and full knowledge of offending behavior. Under other circumstances, children can keep information shared in therapy or an assessment private. In this case, confidentiality cannot apply because the behaviors are harmful to others. This is all explained to the child. The child is also told that honesty is important. A skilled interviewer who has carefully reviewed the file will have a good idea when the child is lying. Remember that many of the children who exhibit these problems have problems with dishonesty.

The assessment then explores all aspects of the offending behavior: who, what, and when. Exactly who the child molested, in what manner, and at what times. The assessment also looks at how the child views the family, family conflicts, and family rules. It covers discipline, punishment, sleeping arrangements, and privacy practices (i.e., bathroom use).

The interviewer is likely to have a different style than a typical therapist or other mental health worker. The style tends to be supportive but firm. Usually there is more confrontation than in a sexual abuse assessment, which would be more supportive and rarely confrontational because these children do not want us to know what types of sexualized activities they have been involved in. If you would like to read more about the adolescent sex offender, there is a review chapter on this topic in Schwartz and Cellini [1997]. Team members need to be aware that the sexually aggressive child may portray the interviewer and/or the therapist to others as abusive or punitive to set up conflicts and to attempt to be released from the assessment or treatment process.

Treatment of the Juvenile Sex Offender

As a point of clarification, "juvenile sex offender" refers to treatment of youths under the age of 18. There is a substantial literature on the treatment of adult sex offenders, some on teenagers who offend, and others that combine the school-age and adolescent groups. Group therapy is the treatment of choice for school-aged and adolescent offenders, because the combination of confrontation and support provided by peers and therapists is optimal. If you do not have this available in your agency, you may need to team with other agencies who provide these services or send staff to get the specialized training. Teaming with other agencies can be advantageous because the other agencies may need children to complete groups so that children of similar ages can receive treatment together. Multiagency efforts are also a good idea because foster parents and mental health professionals can support one another as they do the treatment.

The first step in treating the juvenile sex offender is to teach the child about the "cycle of abuse" [Ryan et al. 1991]. Research has shown that children do not sexually molest others randomly. Rather, there is a distinct cycle that leads to abusive behaviors including the following [Ryan et al. 1991]:

- Trigger event
- Misinterpretation
- Negative expectation
- Feelings of anger
- Power/control behaviors
- Fantasies
- Planning
- Grooming/stalking
- Opportunity to molest
- Sexual assault
- Guilt/fear
- Suppression (pushing feelings away)
- Return to trigger and start cycle again

Here is a clinical example of how the cycle works. A seven-year-old child who molests hears his foster mother tell his sisters to get dressed in their leotards for dance class. The notion of the girls dressing excites him (trigger event). The girls get on their dance clothes and come into the family room, dancing around. The boy views the dancing as a means to antagonize him (misinterpretation). He then starts thinking about the fact that his foster mother must like the girls better because they get to do more fun things (negative expectation) and begins to get furious (anger). He then pushes the girls around and cusses them (power/control behaviors). He begins to envision grabbing their buttocks, imagining how the leotards would feel (fantasies). He begins to develop a plan for getting the younger of the two to hide behind the couch with him (making plans). He stops pushing around the younger sister and whispers things to her like "I like you best" (grooming). He then proposes a fun new game involving hiding behind the couch to the younger girl (opportunity to molest). His sister joins him behind the couch where he molests her (sexual assault). He then feels badly for what he has done and worries she will tell (guilt/fear). He tells himself that it doesn't matter, she is just a stupid sister (pushing feelings away).

Children are taught the model and eventually learn to apply it to their own behavior. The idea is that by learning what situations trigger the cycle for that child, the child (and foster family) can work to avoid high-risk situations, or to interrupt the cycle once it has started. Therapy would also examine ways that the child's life experiences relate to the cycle and teach coping skills. This therapy is one type of cognitive behavior therapy, which teaches the children to identify thinking processes (cognitions) that lead to offending behavior. Goals in group therapy (adapted from Ryan, Lane, & Rinzler [1991]) are listed below:

- To increase accountability for actions and to decrease denial and minimization of sexual offending
- To increase empathy
- To understand one's own "cycle of abuse" and to decrease reliance on a victim role ("poor me")
- To build social skills to decrease isolation and the concept of oneself as deviant or crazy
- To teach about feelings (affective education)
- To increase self-esteem
- To increase self-control
- To increase problem-solving skills, to decrease thinking errors and distorted beliefs (e.g., "She wanted me to do it.")
- To increase anger management
- To learn about sexuality and arousal and to correct inaccurate sexual information
- To learn to accept authority and to decrease use of power and control strategies
- To improve decision-making skills

Children in sexual offender group therapy tend to meet more often than other types of groups. They can benefit from more intensive therapy to decrease the sexual acting out. Group begins with a discussion of rules, confidentiality, and consequences for noncompliance. Therapists explain how confidentiality rules are different in group because the need for safety outweighs the need for confidentiality in this situation. Though such a group may affect school activities of the foster child, it is best to follow the treatment so that safety in the home and community can increase. Often children require other types of therapy, such as family or individual therapy.

Tips for Foster Parents

Gil [1994] presents some excellent tips for foster parents. A summary of her ideas and some of my own follow.

Dealing with public masturbation. We have already discussed varying family views on the topic of masturbation. Briefly, many mental health professionals take the position that masturbating, if not excessive, is normal, though many families feel differently due to cultural or religious beliefs. Sexually aggressive children may show inappropriate masturbating behaviors that are troublesome in the family and community. Gil recommends that requests to refrain from masturbating in public be made in a respectful (e.g., not negative) manner. Children can also be distracted with other activities that would involve the use of their hands, can be offered another activity that is attractive to them, or simply be allowed a private place to masturbate if this fits with the family philosophy.

It is also important to share information about the child's public masturbation with the treatment team so that the group therapists can explore "triggers" and other emotional concerns. For families where masturbation is unacceptable, mental health professionals need to know that no amount of quoting research findings about the normalcy of masturbation will change the parent's thinking. What can be successful is simply stating to the child that masturbation is not allowed in the family.

Training Exercise: Dealing with Public Masturbation

Practice by role-playing different ways a parent could tell a child not to masturbate in public. Practice what to do when it happens, as well as how to talk about it later on.

Sexual aggression toward others. The level of supervision should be carefully assessed prior to placement, according to Gil. We all know that children are often placed without the foster family knowing that the child has this problem. In this case, the treatment team needs to determine what level of supervision the child needs and how to attain this level of supervision. It is often the case that members of the treatment team are in agreement that the child needs almost constant supervision around other children, yet the child is placed in a foster home with several other foster and/or biological children.

Perhaps the foster parent is a single mother. She has to go to work, prepare meals, do laundry, give kids baths, and so forth. In this scenario, how could she provide "constant supervision"? One foster mother came up with a good solution. She had four kids and one was sexually aggressive. All of the kids were aware of the sexually aggressive child's problems. She instituted a reward system for telling on certain negative behaviors, including sexual ones. All the kids were rewarded for telling. What happened was that the children generally reported on the offender so he could not sexually perpetrate. Another tough issue is reducing this child's access to victims. A good number of foster families have a home business of baby-sitting. There needs to be some careful thought into how to keep young children safe from older, sexually acting-out children.

Sexual talk around peers. In addition to actually touching other children in a sexual manner, these children do a lot of sexually suggestive gesturing, sexualized talk, and jokes. They may dance in sexy ways or eat food in a sexualized manner. First, you need to scrutinize the child's environment to be sure that sexual imagery is minimized. (This is discussed in Chapter 1).

Sleeping arrangements. Children who molest cannot sleep in the same room with other children. We run into a few problems with this one. Suppose the child is placed in the home before it is known he is an offender. Suppose there are five children in the family—two girls and three boys—and there is a girls' room and a boys' room. The child cannot sleep in another room (i.e., on the living room couch) because foster care rules state that each child must have a bed and a room. It may not be the best thing to have the child sleep in the parents' room if this could be overstimulating. Plus, the parents may feel they need their privacy. Now you have a king-sized dilemma.

Gil suggests that the child be isolated until the child can control him/herself or sleep with children who can protect themselves (e.g., because they are much older, for example). There are no easy answers here because there are practical issues of space in the home, availability of another home that is suitable for the child, and foster care rules. A good place to start, however, is for the treatment team to discuss sleeping arrangements and supervision openly. In a small number of cases where children "roam the house" at night, the foster parents installed a laser sensor on the child's door so they would be aware when the child who molested left his room.

Hygiene. Children who molest cannot use the bathroom or bathe with other children. Period. Team members must pay careful attention to bathroom practices in the school. A child with this problem, for example, may not be able to go to the bathroom when the whole class goes and may need to go when no one else is in the bathroom. Team members may need to make special arrangements for the child to use a bathroom with only one toilet.

Unsupervised peer activities. Children who molest cannot "go outside and play" like other children, without supervision. If they are not supervised, they will find opportunities to molest other children. This creates a dilemma for the parent who depends on the kids playing outside to get a few things done. Providing round-the-clock supervision is a team issue. We want these children to have experiences with peers, but they need close supervision to do so.

Sexualized behavior with foster parents. What is the thing to do if a foster child touches the foster parent in a sexualized way? Petersen, Magee, and Muher [1993] recommend saying the following: "I want a hug with real feelings" or "In this family, kids and parents don't share grown-up touching." Many foster parents are sexually "nuzzled" by particularly young children, say three to five, without recognizing the sexual nature of these behaviors. The child may burrow into the mother's chest or midsection, or sit next to the foster parent and bury his or her head in the foster parent's lap or by the buttocks. Some foster parents misinterpret these behaviors as awkward attempts at affection. In a baby, they are, but a three-year-old is old enough to know this is not an appropriate way to show affection. It is *extremely* important to label these behaviors as sexual. A child who is not a molester, if told that touching the mother's breasts is inappropriate, will generally stop doing it. If the child is not stopped, there is a problem [see Johnson 1998].

Other ideas

Get a copy of T. C. Johnson's *Helping Children with Sexual Behavior Problem*, which maps out specific strategies for parents and substitute caregivers for dealing with sexually inappropriate behaviors and gives more detail than what was included here. Also look at the booklet *From Trauma to Understanding: A Guide for Parents of Children with Sexual Behavior Problems* listed in the Resources section.

The most important thing foster parents can do as members of the treatment team for children who molest is to be able to hear what the child is saying. Until we believe and accept that the child does disgusting, heinous, hurtful sexual things to others, he or she will not be helped. If the foster parents do not believe little Johnny is sticking things up his sister's vagina, then he will keep doing it. Treatment team members need to support one another to come to terms with the severity and cruelty of what these children do, even very small children. When one foster mother learned that her six-year-old foster daughter was molesting her four-year-old brother, she said that both she and her baby-sitter "had a feeling" that something was not right, but did not know what it was. Trust these feelings.

Another important issue is how to divide parent time between the offender and the victim when they both live under the same roof. Gil [1994] points out that families may need special help in these circumstances to deal with such questions as: Should you talk to the children separately or together about what happened? How can they have a normal brother-sister (or brother-brother, or sister-sister) relationship after one molested the other?

Another thing to keep in mind is that these children can be difficult to work with. They can make us uncomfortable. Veteran therapists have had ten-year-old children request sex with them, three-year-olds pinch their buttocks, and had children masturbate in front of them. We cannot help but have our own feelings about these experiences and need to get support from our peers to make some sense of it. This introduces the topic of the next chapter: how to best take care of ourselves, as people who care for children with sexualized behaviors.

7

The Emotional Cost of Working with Sexually Traumatized Children

Mental health professionals and foster parents often view themselves as competent people who care deeply about children. We see ourselves helping children to achieve a better life and happiness. Over time, we learn that our ability to help depends heavily on the family of origin, the judicial system, the social services system, and a myriad of other factors. This realization can have a profound effect on our self-view as helpers. We struggle to make sense of the many ways people hurt children. It shakes our own beliefs of the world as a decent place. People who work with child sexual abuse survivors may experience increased personal vulnerability, a heightened sense of fear, and hypervigilance. We are at risk personally, socially, and professionally as we try to integrate what we do with our own histories and life experiences [Ryan et al. 1991].

On a daily basis, many of us are aware of the cruel and sadistic things people do to children. In fact, Ryan, Lane, & Rinzler [1991] describe the impact of providing sexual abuse treatment as similar to the impact of sexual abuse itself. They list a number of ways we react to illustrate this point:

- **Denial**: "No one would do that to a child."
- **Rationalization**: "The mother had a lot of problems so she couldn't protect her kids."
- **Secrecy/avoidance**: "Do we have to talk about this?"
- **Disbelief**: "He couldn't have raped her; she is only three years old."
- **Blaming the victim**: "She acts like a slut; she asked for it."

The sad part about all of this is that those of us in mental health have worked really hard not to accept that sexual abuse treatment has an effect on us. It's like coal miners convincing themselves that inhaling the coal dust is good for them, or like window washers who believe they could never fall off the scaffolding. Sometimes it happens. We go on thinking we are invincible. We do not study the phenomenon and few of us write about it.

The bottom line is that we all can experience burnout. Burnout can lead us to make mistakes in our work: a foster parent spanks a child for exposing herself, a therapist does not follow the treatment goal to address sexual abuse because he cannot take it anymore, a case worker stops asking and listening to foster parents' reports that the kids are humping each other. Burnout can also make us quit our jobs. With the relatively small number of individuals trained for this special population, we cannot afford to lose the foster parents and mental health professionals who are good at it. (On the other hand, if a person is not emotionally equipped to do the job, it's best they try something else.)

Let's start with how to recognize burnout (adapted from Ryan et al. [1991]). If you are burned out, you are likely to experience some, but not all, of the following:

- You have a lot of aches and pains.
- You are always tired.
- You just can't seem to get going.
- You lose your appetite for food, sex, and social contact.
- You start spending less time on your job (if you're a foster parent, you spend less time with the foster kids; if you're a mental health professional, you spend less time on your cases, minimizing contact with the foster parent, child, and team members).
- You are apathetic.
- You have lowered expectations; you think the child will never get better, so why bother?
- You feel detached.
- You feel depressed.
- The longer this goes on, the more you deny that you have a problem.
- You use drugs, alcohol, food, or sex to make yourself feel better.

One subject that we absolutely do not want to talk about or perhaps to acknowledge is the effect that sexual abuse treatment has on our own sexuality. We become accustomed to abuse concerns in a way that makes us question whether we are normal sexually [Ryan & Lane 1991]. Supervisors do not ask therapists or case managers if they experience deviations in their sex drive, for example. Nor do team members ask foster parents whether their sex life is affected by the sexually deviant events that occur in their homes. We will continue not to ask one another these questions, because we all need to maintain privacy boundaries. We know that problems can and do exist, however; Ryan, Lane, & Rinzler [1991] learned through questionnaires that sex offender therapists have experiences of disinterest in sex, increased arousal, or deviant sexual imagery. We can respond to this problem by training individuals to explore for themselves the adverse effects that sexual abuse treatment work can have on sexuality.

Now, troubled clinicians have the luxury of going home at the end of a workday to "get a break" from the sexual business. Research articles on burnout always recommend getting away from the source of the stress. Foster parents, however, have a kind of stress no one else has on the team: they cannot get away from it. Even when they have respite care— say a weekend when the child is cared for by another foster parent— there can be nagging doubts about whether the behaviors will be managed appropriately, whether the child is molesting another child, or whether the child will return home acting worse. The foster parents can come to feel that the temporary relief of respite care is not worth the worries. When they go on vacation, usually the foster child goes on vacation, too. It is surprising that no research on foster parents' stress relating to sexual abuse treatment is evident in the extensive literature search undertaken for this book. This is an important phenomenon to understand, because it is possible that factors relating to this type of unrelenting stress affect whether the child can remain in the home. The extent to which foster parent burnout affects placement disruption is unknown.

Foster parents routinely have to change family practices to accommodate the sexually abused child. Foster parents often have to put items that provoke sexualized behavior out of reach. One foster mother had to put her makeup out of reach, because the child would apply makeup in a sexualized manner and strut provocatively with the makeup on. Other foster parents cannot embrace or cuddle in the room while they are watching TV late at night because the foster child awakens and watches them. Foster parents have learned that foster children listen at the door when they are having sex. One grandmotherly foster mother had three- and five-year-old children who looked up her skirts; she began wearing slacks. Foster parents can be embarrassed by the sexualized acts of the child; neighbors and friends may observe and misunderstand these behaviors. Neighbors, family, and friends may pressure them to "get rid of those kids" when they observe their behaviors. Foster parents wonder if they are doing a good job. They neglect their own needs, because they are so busy taking care of others.

To add another stressor, foster parents and other mental health professionals have reported difficulties working with birth family members because they have negative feelings about the parent who was abusive or was neglectful in a way that allowed the child to be abused. This can create loyalty conflicts for the foster child, which will impede treatment. Barth and colleagues [1994] developed foster parent training on childhood sexual abuse to alleviate these problems. The series of specialized training sessions also allows foster parents to develop a support group of people dealing with similar problems.

If the child is sexually aggressive, it is thought that parents' acceptance of the problem makes the parents feel as if they have suffered a loss. Pithers et al. [1993] talks about how parents go through these five stages of loss associated with the loss of a loved one: denial, anger, bargaining, depression, and acceptance. Also, if the child is sexually aggressive, the birth family may blame the foster family for "causing" this problem, or the foster family blames the birth family as the root of the problem. All of these conflicting emotions can take their toll.

Finally, as we do this type of work, we grow accustomed to hearing about bad things kids and adults do to kids. We worry more and we get a little paranoid. One therapist experienced anxiety about finding a babysitter for her children on occasional evenings. The criteria she used to manage the anxiety was that the sitter had to be a female from families she knew from church. Then she would pay the sitter to come the first time while she was there to observe her behavior with the children (ostensibly so the sitter could get to know the children). We check our doors more, may carry a weapon, or are overly cautious in some way. We have trouble trusting people. As Ryan, Lane, & Rinzler [1991] point out, fear of the known is sometimes worse than fear of the unknown.

What to Do About Emotional Overload

The following strategies can lessen the emotional burden we bear from working with this challenging group of children and teenagers.

- Be aware of the problem. Train staff to recognize the problem. Assure staff that they will not be penalized or lose their jobs for getting help.
- Work with your team. This helps to reduce feelings of isolation and provides a forum for problem solving.

- Create a supportive environment in the foster care program.
- Acknowledge or accept the very slow rate of clinical change in the treatment of sexually abused and sexually offending children.
- Employ good stress management.
- Get ongoing training about sexual abuse and sexual aggression.
- Admit you are burned out.
- Take care of yourself. It sounds like a cliché, but Pithers et al. [1993] recommends doing something to relax daily, like taking a bath, getting exercise, reading, or talking with friends.
- If you are married, take care of your marriage.
- If you are a foster parent, you need respite. Discuss options with the team.
- If you are a therapist/case manager, think about how to use your personal time or vacation time.
- Spend some time with nonclinical groups of children so you can retain some sense of normalcy.
- If you are an abuse survivor, be sure that you can do this kind of work and get treatment if you need it.

Let's discuss a few of these.

Support. Just as we recommend support for survivors, it's a good idea to build in supports for all of us. We do not all need to run out and get therapy. Support can mean talking about the problems with treatment team members and supporting one another. It means being able to tactfully share with a colleague if you are getting "over the edge" on a case. Discuss difficult cases with colleagues: foster parents seek out other foster parents in training meetings with similar problems, social workers and therapists look for peers at training and conferences, and so forth. Foster parents have said that talking with another foster parent who is going through some of the same challenges can be helpful. It may lead to the sharing of ideas that could then be shared with the treatment team before implementation.

Stress management. Do the best you can with your own stress management. Begin to think of yourself as a person with high levels of stress who needs a plan to keep yourself healthy. Foster parents and mental health workers can function like superheroes. They are used to being everything for everybody. We all know this is not healthy, and we should take breaks to do our best. This means respite care if you are a foster parent and vacation time if you are a worker.

Marriages and relationships. Anecdotal evidence by foster parents and therapists indicates that working with the sexually abused child can be hard on a marriage. The book *Preparing for Success* [Peterson et al. 1993] talks about these effects on the marital relationship and what to do about it. The authors recommend strengthening your relationship by good communication and arranging for special time together. This can be a challenge in foster care when respite is hard to get. They also suggest you use your spouse to explore your early life experiences and how they relate to your being a foster parent. The same could be said for therapists.

Abuse survivors. The percentage of foster parents, therapists, social workers, and other mental health professionals working with sexually abused foster children who were themselves abused at some point in their life is unknown. Anyone who works in mental health can tell you, however, that people gravitate to the profession for a variety of reasons, and one of them may have to do with the professional's history of abuse. Ryan, Lane, & Rinzler [1991] reported a study where participants at a child abuse conference were asked to indicate whether they were survivors of abuse; a whopping 45% had a history of childhood sexual abuse. Abuse survivors may not tell others on the treatment team of their history.

If you have sat on a treatment team or two, there have probably been times when you wondered whether a colleague had an abuse history from the things she or he said or did. We do not want to get into the position of psychoanalyzing one another on treatment teams. People need their privacy. This being said, we need to operate on the honor system on this one. If you are an abuse survivor, take care of your own personal psychological business. Being an abuse survivor carries both positive and negative effects. On the one hand, an abuse survivor can uniquely understand the abused child's perspective. On the other hand, a history of abusive experiences can make the abused foster parent or mental health professional susceptible to posttraumatic stress reactions triggered by the children they care for.

It's not a good idea to be doing this work to "make up for" your own hurts or as a means of retaliation. Look at yourself to be sure you are not putting your feelings about your own abuse on the child you are treating. Evaluate whether speaking or hearing about their abuse experiences somehow causes you to relive your own trauma. This is called "vicarious traumatization" [Ryan et al. 1991]. Figure out how to get your personal stuff out of the treatment of the child. This may involve getting therapy.

If those of us working in foster care increased our sensitivity to the stress that working with sexually abused children places upon us, we will be able to train and support one another more effectively. It is my opinion, after years of working on foster care treatment teams, that the person with the highest level of stress is the foster parent, who is also the one who spends the most time with the child and gets paid the least of the members on the team.

8

Directions for the Future

Working with sexually abused children in foster care is noble, but exhausting work. Creating an atmosphere where sexuality can be discussed openly will make the job easier. Developing good working relationships with team members, regardless of differing levels of experience, cultural background, and such, will also make the job easier for everyone.

We are at some disadvantage in foster care because researchers in sexual abuse have not been interested in this subpopulation of the larger population of sexually abused children. It is possible that this important area has been neglected because doing research in foster care can be difficult. Staff must always put the child's welfare and safety first, so filling out forms or completing extra paperwork is not welcome. It is also hard to study our population because research can get messy. We are not just dealing with a group of sexually abused children. We are talking about a group of multiply abused children, often with poor documentation about their mistreatment—children living in extreme poverty and chaos with many definable "risk factors."

Those of us who work in foster care need to give some thought as to how we can make research a bigger priority and how we can accommodate the demands of the researcher in our frenetic schedules. At the top of our list, we need some good studies to tell us how many sexually abused children are serviced in foster care programs.

I would recommend that foster care programs train repeatedly and often on the topic of sexual abuse. New research brings with it more assessment tools and treatment strategies every five years or so. For example, for years it was thought that sexually abused children had low self-esteem and this should be a priority in treatment. Research shows that actually few sexually abused children are rated as having low self-esteem by parents; other factors are much more problematic. Teaching about normative sexuality also needs to be incorporated in sexual abuse training programs. Agencies could benefit from interagency coordination of training and service delivery, as in the case of sexual abuse groups mentioned in Chapter 5.

Developing a core of foster parents and clinicians who specialize in work with sexually abused children in foster care will be highly advantageous for the children we serve. There will always be children who have been placed in a nonspecialist home, but who turn out to have been sexually abused. In those cases, foster parents with more expertise might mentor foster parents with less experience. Therapists, too, need to be trained to work with foster children and foster families more effectively. Administrators need to identify obstacles to teaming and develop plans for alleviating long-standing conflicts among different professionals who treat foster children.

Strategies for involving the birth families need to be integrated into treatment approaches. Reunification is unlikely to be successful if the birth family members have not been involved closely in sexual abuse treatment. In particular, treatment for the sexually aggressive child in foster care who is transitioning back to the community needs to be developed.

Foster care programs need to develop a library of materials like the ones listed in the resource section. Often a research grant can be obtained to upgrade a program's library or staff time devoted to researching materials at a nearby university library. I would recommend starting with the following materials and expanding as budgets allow:

- One good current text on sexual abuse. There are many good ones out there and several are listed in the references. Every five years or so, you will need to replace it with a more current version. Check that the book has a good section on PTSD.

- Foster parent and staff training materials. Try Mars [1999], Johnson [1998a, 1998b] and Pithers et al. [1993] for starters.

- Several children's therapeutic books on sexual abuse. Check with your therapists to see what they have in their libraries and might be willing to share. There is a list of these books in the back, which can be ordered from bookstores, catalogs, or the Internet. If you find that these books are out of print, look at professional conferences for contemporary books on this topic.

- Resources on the sexually aggressive child and teenager.

- One good videotape on sexual abuse.

  One book I particularly recommend is *Assessing Allegations of Child*

Sexual Abuse by K. Kuehnle, listed in the Reference section. This is an impressive book on sexual abuse assessment, with great resources throughout the book and in the appendix. If you find it difficult to obtain, look in local universities or community colleges.

While you are getting your library together, look into sources of funds for more staff and foster parents to attend state, local, and national conferences on child sexual abuse. Their job will be to pick up more resources for the library and report back to the agency about new developments in the field. One means of funding is to write a small grant to incorporate both the library idea and money for conferences to develop more sophisticated programming in the agency for sexually abused foster children. You can also gain information on new developments by attending local meetings. If you contact the organizations on the list in the references, you can find out if they have local chapters and when they meet.

We need to be realistic when we train new foster parents, therapists, social workers, case managers, and so forth about the realities of working with the sexually abused child. For foster parents, the review has shown that school-aged abused children are the most difficult, followed by preschoolers, and then teenagers. Foster parents need to know the high levels of supervision these children will require. They need to know how hard it will be to achieve that level of supervision in some families.

Therapists, social workers, and other mental health professionals need to know that teamwork is required for this type of work. If staff are accustomed to being "the expert" by virtue of training and degrees, this thinking will undermine successful team functioning. Supervisors need to be able to address not only the clinical issues their staff struggle with, but also the issues of stress management and socioemotional distress. They need to be trained to notice this problem in their staff and how to make recommendations in a way that will respect the staff members' privacy. Finally, foster care directors must be aware of these concerns so that they can allocate funds for programming accordingly.

It is an exciting time to be providing services to sexually abused children in foster care, because we have the resources and the technology to help children with these difficult problems. Providing this help will not come easily to most of us, however, for it has a high cost and sometimes limited rewards. It is my hope that this book will help those who use it to continue doing their best with a group of challenging children who deserve our caring and expertise.

Resources

Books on Sexuality Education

Bourgeois, P., Wolfish, M., & Martyn, K. (1994). *Changes in you and me: A book about puberty, mostly for boys*. Kansas City, MO: Andrews McMeel Publishing.

Bourgeois, P. & Wolfish, M. (1994). *Changes in you and me: A book about puberty, mostly for girls*. Kansas City, MO: Andrews McMeel Publishing.

Cyprian, J. (1998). *Teaching human sexuality: A guide for parents and other caregivers*. Washington, DC: CWLA Press.

Fenwick, E. & Walker, R. (1994). *How sex works: A clear comprehensive guide for teenagers to emotional, physical and sexual maturity*. New York: Dorling Kindersley.

Gravelle, K., Gravelle, J, & D. Palen. (1996). *The period book: Everything you don't want to ask (but need to know)*. New York: Walker & Co.

Harris, R. H. (1994). *It's perfectly normal: A book about changing bodies, growing up, sex and sexual health*. Cambridge, MA: Candlewick Press.

Johnson, T. C. (1998). *Understanding children's sexual behavior: What's normal and healthy*. Available from the author at 1101 Fremont Avenue, Suite 1101, S. Pasedena, CA 91030.

Madaras, L., Saavedra, D., & Lopez, R. (1987). *The "What's Happening to My Body?" workbook for boys*. New York: Newmarket Press.

Madaras, L. & Madaras, A. (1993). *My body, myself*. New York: Newmarket Press.

Madaras, L. & Madaras, A. (1995). *The "What's Happening to My Body?" workbook for girls*. New York: Newmarket Press.

Marsh, C. S. (1989). *Sex stuff for kids 7-17*. Bath, NC: Gallopade Publishing Group.

Marsh, C.S. (1989). *Smart sex stuff for kids workbook*. Bath, NC: Gallopade Publishing Group.

Pithers, W. D., Gray, A. S., Cunningham, C., & Lane, S. (1993). *From trauma to understanding: A guide for parents of children with sexual behavior problems*. Brandon, VT: The Safer Society Program and Press, P. O. Box 340 Brandon, VT 05733.

Somers, L. & Somers, B. C. (1989). *Talking to your children about love & sex*. Markham, Ontario: New American Library.

Wiehe, V. R. (1997). *Sibling abuse: Hidden physical, emotional, and sexual trauma*. Thousand Oaks, CA: Sage Publications.

Books for Children Who Are Abuse Survivors

Baird, K. (1986). *My body belongs to me*. Pines, MN: American Guidance Service, Inc.

Bernstein, S. C. & Ritz, K. (1991). *A family that fights*. Morton Grove, IL: Albert Whitman & Co.

Blank, J. & Quackenbush, M. (1980). *The playbook for kids about sex*. Burlingame, CA: YES Press.

Channing Bete, Inc. (1986). *What every kid should know about sexual abuse*. South Deerfield, MA: Channing Bete, Inc.

Freed, K. S. (1985) *Red flag, green flag people: A personal safety program for children*. Workbook and coloring book. Fargo-Moorhead, MN: Rape and Abuse Crisis Center.

Freeman, L. (1983). *It's my body*. Seattle, WA: Parenting Press.

Gil, E. & Haskell, S. (1986). *I told my secret: A book for kids who were abused.* Walnut Creek, CA: Launch Press.

Girard, L. W. (1984). *My body is private.* New York: Albert Whitman & Co.

Hindeman, J. (1983). *A very touching book... For little people and for big people.* Durkee, OR: McClure-Hindman Associates.

Mars, B. L. (1999). *Bobbie's story: A feelings workbook.* Washington, DC: CWLA Press.

Mosen, A. & Meton, P. (1991). Don't feed the monster on Tuesday: The children's self-esteem book. Plainview, NY: Childswork Childsplay.

Russell, P. & Stone, B. (1986). *Do you have a secret?* Minneapolis, MN: Complare Publishers.

Stanek, M. (1987). *Don't hurt me Mama.* Morton Grove, IL: Albert Whitman & Co.

Video

For Adults

Breaking Silence
Future Educational Films
1628 Union Street
San Francisco, CA 94123

Child Molestation: Breaking the Silence
Coronet/MTI Film & Video
108 Wilmot Rd.
Deerfield, IL 60015
800/777-2400

Confronting Child Sexual Abuse: A Video Training Series
Introduction by Oprah Winfrey
Child Welfare League of America
440 First Street NW, Third Floor
Washington, DC   20001-2085
800/407-6273
Fax: 301/206-9789

How to Tell if a Child is Being Abused
Bureau for At-Risk Youth
645 New York Avenue
Huntington, NY 11743
800/999-6884

*Identifying, Reporting, & Handling Disclosure of the Sexually
Abused Child*
Committee for Children
172 20th Ave.
Seattle, WA 98122-5862
800/634-4449

The Last Taboo
Coronet/MTI Film & Video
108 Wilmot Road
Deerfield, IL 60015
800/777-2400

For Children

Believe Me
Coronet/MTI Film & Video
188 Wilmot Road
Deerfield, IL 60015
800/777-2400

Safety Protection Tips from a Professional Crime Prevention Educator
Childswork Childsplay
P. O. Box 1604
Secaucus, NJ 07096-1604
800/962-1141

Shrug: Self-worth
Secret Adventure Video Series #SA994
By Michael Smith
Marco Products, Inc., Dept. F99
1443 Old York Road
Warminster, PA 18974

Games

Kids Count Game
Marco Products, Inc.
1443 Old York Road
Warminster, PA 18974

Organizations

American Academy of Child and Adolescent Psychiatry
3615 Wisconsin Avenue NW
Washington, DC 20016-3007
202/966-7300
Fax: 202/966-2891
www.aacap.org

American Association for Protecting Children
63 Inverness Drive East
Englewood, CO 80112-5117
800/227-5242

American Professional Society on the Abuse of Children (APSC)
407 S. Dearborn Street, Suite 1300
Chicago, IL 60605
312/554-0166
www.apsac.org

Child Welfare League of America
440 First Street NW, Third Floor
Washington, DC   20001-2085
202/942-2952
Fax: 202/638-4004
www.cwla.org

Foster Family-Based Treatment Association (FFTA)
1415 Queen Anne Road
Teaneck, NJ, 07666
800/414-FFTA (3382)
www.ffta.org

National Center on Child Abuse and Neglect (NCCAN)
(sponsors the National Clearinghouse on Child Abuse and
Neglect)
P.O. Box 1182
Washington, DC 20013
www.calib.com/nccanch

National Resource Center on Child Sexual Abuse
107 Lincoln Street
Huntsville, AL 35801
1-800-KIDS-006.

Prevent Child Abuse America
P. O. Box 2866
Chicago, IL 60690-9950
www.childabuse.org

SIECUS
130 W. 42nd Street, Suite 350
New York, NY 10036
www.siecus.org

Resources for Assessment Instruments

Anxiety Disorders Interview Schedule for Children, Revised
Graywind Publications
c/o Center for Stress and Anxiety Disorders
1535 Western Avenue
Albany, NY 12203

Child Behavior Checklist
University of Vermont
Department of Psychiatry
1 South Prospect Street
Burlington, VT 05401
802/656-8313
http://Checklist.uvm.edu

Child Sexual Behavior Inventory
Psychological Assessment, 4(3), 303-311, (September 1992)

Conners Rating Scales
Multi-Health Systems
908 Niagara Falls Boulevard
North Tonawanda, NY 14120-2060

Devereux Scales of Mental Disorders
Psychological Corporation
555 Academic Court
San Antonio, TX 78204-2498

Draw a Person: Screening Procedure for Emotional Disturbance
Pro-Ed
8700 Shoal Creek Boulevard
Austin, TX 78758

Personality Inventory for Children, Revised Format
Western Psychological Services
12031 Wilshire Boulevard
Los Angeles, CA 90025

Stress Impact Scale
Pro-Ed
8700 Shoal Creek Boulevard
Austin, TX 78758

Trauma Symptom Checklist
John Briere
Department of Psychiatry and the Behavioral Sciences
University of Southern California Medical Center
1934 Hospital Place
Los Angeles, CA 90033-1071

References

Achenbach, T. M. (1991). *Manual for the Child Behavior Checklist/4–18 and 1991 profile.* Burlington: University of Vermont, Department of Psychiatry.

Achenbach, T. M. (1992). *Manual for the Child Behavior Checklist/2–3 and 1992 profile.* Burlington: University of Vermont, Department of Psychiatry.

Barth, R. P., Yeaton, J., & Winterfelt, N. (1994). Psychoeducational groups with foster parents of sexually abused children. *Child and Adolescent Social Work Journal, 11(5),* 405–424.

Bellak, L. (1993). *The T.A.T., C.A.T. and S.A.T. in clinical use (5th edition).* Needham Heights, MA: Allyn & Bacon.

Berliner, L. & Ernst, E. (1984). Group work with preadolescent assalt victims. In I. R. Short & J. G. Greer (Eds.), *Victims of sexual aggression: Treatment of children, women, and men (pp. 105–126). New York: Van Nostrand Reinhold.*

Bourgeois, P. & Wolfish, M. (1994). *Changes in you and me: A book about puberty, mostly for girls.* Kansas City, MO: Andrews McMeel Publishing.

Briere, J. (1989). *Trauma Symptom Checklist.* Los Angeles: Author.

Briere, J. N. & Elliot, D. M. (1994). Immediate and long-term impacts of child sexual abuse. *The Future of Children: Sexual Abuse of Children, 4(2),* 54–69.

Browne, A. & Finkelhor, D. (1986). The impact of child sexual abuse: A review of the research. *Psychological Bulletin, 99,* 66–77.

Buck, J. N. (1970). *The House-Tree-Person Technique, revised manual.* Los Angeles: Western Psychological Services.

Conners, C. K. (1997). *The Conners Rating Scales.* North Tonawanda, NY: Multi-Health Systems.

Dunn, W. J. *(1998). You, self-esteem & dreams.* Warminister, PA: Marco Products, Inc.

Exner, J. E. (1986). *The Rorschach: A comprehensive system. Volume 1: Basic Foundations (2nd edition).* New York: John Wiley & Sons.

Faller, K. C. (1988). *Child sexual abuse: An interdisciplinary manual for diagnosis, case management, and treatment.* New York: Columbia University Press.

Finkelhor, D. (1981). *Sexually victimized children.* New York: Free Press.

Finkelhor, D., Hotaling, G., Lewis, I. A., & Smith, C. (1990). Sexual abuse in a national study of adult men and women: Prevalence, characteristics and risk factors. *Child Abuse & Neglect, 14,* 19–28.

Foster Family-Based Treatment Association [FFTA]. (1996). *Status of treatment foster care in North America.* Teaneck, NJ: Author.

Friedrich, W. N., Grambsch, P., Damon, L., Hewitt, S. K., Koverola, C., Lang, R., & Wolfe, V. (1992). The Child Sexual Behavior Inventory. *Psychological Assessment, 4*(3), 303–311.

Gardner, R. A. (1998). *The talking, feeling, doing game.* Cresskill, NJ: Creative Therapeutics.

Garcia-de la Rocha, B. (1989). *Identifying and managing the behavior of the sexually abused child: Final report.* Washington, DC: U.S. Department of Health and Human Development Service.

Gil, E. (1991). *A guide for young sex offenders.* Walnut Creek, CA: Launch Press.

Gil, E. (1994). Out-of-home care for children who molest. In J. McNamera (Ed.), *Sexually reactive children in adoption and foster care* (pp. 129–133). Greensboro, NC: Family Resources.

Gomes-Schwartz, B. (1990). *Child sexual abuse: The initial effects.* Beverly Hills, CA: Sage Publications.

Gomes-Schwartz, B., Horowitz, J. M., & Sauzier, M. (1985). Severity of emotional distress among sexually abused preschool, school-aged, and adolescent children. *Hospital and Community Psychiatry, 36,* 503–508.

Goodman, G. S. & Aman, C. (1990). Children's use of anatomically detailed dolls to recount an event. *Child Development, 61,* 1859–1871.

Haffner, D. W. (1999). *From diapers to dating: A parent's guide to raising sexually healthy children.* New York: Newmarket Press.

Henry, D., Cossett, D., Auletta, T., & Eagan, E. (1991). Needed Services for Foster Parenting Sexually Abused Children. *Child and Adolescent Social Work Journal, 8*(2), 127–140.

Hicks, B. (1999). *Kids Count Game.* Warminster, PA: Marco Products, Inc.

Hobbs, C. J. , Hanks, H. G. I., & Wynne, J. M. (1993). *Child abuse and neglect: A clinician's handbook.* London: Churchill Livingstone.

Johnson, T. C. (1991, August/September). Understanding the sexual behavior of young children. *IECUS Report.* Available from the author at 1101 Fremont Avenue, Suite 1101, S. Pasedena, CA 91030.

Johnson, T. C. (1998a). Child Sexual Behavior Checklist (CSBCL), (2nd ed.). In T. C. Johnson (Ed.), *Treatment exercises for abused children and children with sexual behavior problems* (pp. 41–46). Available from the author at 1101 Fremont Avenue, Suite 1101, S. Pasedena, CA 91030.

Johnson, T. C. (1998b). *Helping children with sexual behavior problems: A guidebook for parents and caregivers.* Available from the author at 1101 Fremont Avenue, Suite 1101, S. Pasedena, CA 91030.

Johnson, T. C. & Berry, C. (1989). Children who molest: A treatment program. *Journal of Interpersonal Violence, 4*(2), 185–203.

Kendall-Tackett, K. A., Williams, L. M., & Finkelhor, D. (1993). Impact of sexual abuse on children: A review and synthesis of recent empirical studies. *Psychological Bulletin, 113*(1), 164–180.

Kinnear, K. L. (1995). *Childhood sexual abuse: A reference handbook*. Contemporary World Issues series. Santa Barbara, CA: ABC-Clio.

Kruczek, T., & Vitanza, S. (1999). Treatment effects with an adolescent abuse survivor group. *Child Abuse and Neglect, 5,* 477–485.

Kuehnle, K. (1996). *Assessing allegations of child sexual abuse*. Sarasota, FL: Professional Resource Press.

Lie, G. & McMurty, S. C. (1991). Foster care for sexually abused children: A comparative study. *Child Abuse and Neglect, 15,* 111–121.

Madaras, L. & Madaras, A. (1993). *My body, myself*. New York: Newmarket Press.

Mars, B. L. (1999). *Bobbie's story: A guide for foster parents*. Washington, DC: CWLA Press.

Marvasti, A. (1989). Play therapy with sexually abused children. In S. Sgroi (Ed.), *Vulnerable populations. Volume 2* (pp. 1–41). New York: Lexington Books.

Naglieri, J. A., LeBuffe, P. A., & Pfeiffer, S. T. (1994). *Devereux Scales of Mental Disorders*. San Antonio: The Psychological Corporation.

Ormond, M., Durham, D., Leggett, A., & Keating, J. (1998). *Treating the aftermath of sexual abuse: A handbook for working with children in care*. Washington, DC: CWLA Press.

Petersen, C., Magee, V., & Neuber, K. (1993). Preparing for success: A guide for parents who adopt sexually abused children. Springfield, IL: State of Illinois, Department of Children and Family Services.

Pithers, W. D., Gray, A. S., Cunningham, C., & Lane, S. (1993). *From trauma to understanding: A guide for parents of children with sexual behavior problems*. Brandon, VT: The Safer Society Program and Press, P. O. Box 340 Brandon, VT 05733.

Poland, D. C. & Groze, V. (1993). Effects of foster care placement on biological children in the home. *Child and Adolescent Social Work Journal, 10,* 153–164.

Putnam, F. W. (1990). *Child Dissociative Checklist (Version 3.0 – 2/90)*. Bethesda, MD: National Institute of Mental Health, Laboratory of Developmental Psychology.

Pynoos, R. S., Frederick, C., Nader, K., Arroyo, W., Steinberg, S., Eth, S., Nunez, F. & Fairbanks, L. (1987). Life threat and posttraumatic stress in school-aged children. *Archives of General Psychiatry, 44,* 1057–1063.

Reeker, J. & Ensing, D. (1998). An evaluation of a group treatment for sexually abused young children. *Journal of Child Sexual Abuse, 7*(2), 65–85.

Ryan, G., Lane, S., & Rinzler, A. (1991). The impact of sexual abuse on the interventionist. In G. Ryan & S. Lane (Eds.), *Juvenile sexual offending: Causes, consequences, and correction* (pp. 411–428). Lexington, MA: Lexington Books.

Schwartz, B. K. & Cellini, H. R. (1997). *The sex offender: New insights, treatment innovations and legal developments.* Volume II. Kingston, NJ: Civic Research Institute.

Sgroi, S. M., Bunk, B. S., & Wabrek, C. J. (1988). Children's sexual behaviors and their relationship to sexual abuse. In S. M. Sgroi (Ed.). *Vulnerable populations: Evaluation and treatment of sexually abused children and adult survivors. Volume 1* (pp. 1–24). Lexington, MA: Lexington Books.

Shapiro, L. E. (1994). *Short-term therapy with children.* King of Prussia, PA: The Center for Applied Psychology, Inc.

Somers, L. & Somers, B. C. (1989). *Talking to your children above love & sex.* Markham, Ontario: New American Library.

Sorenson, T. & Snow, B. (1991). How children tell: The process of disclosure in child sexual abuse. *Child Welfare, 1*(3), 13.

Thompson, R. W., Authier, K., & Ruma, P. (1994). Behavior problems of sexually abused children in foster care: A preliminary study. *Journal of Child Sexual Abuse, 3*(4), 79–91.

Treacy, E. C. & Fisher, C. B. (1993). Foster parenting the sexually abused: A family life education program. *Journal of Child Sexual Abuse, 2*(1), 47–63.

U.S. Department of Health and Human Services (HHS). (1995). *The national survey of current and former foster parents.* Washington, DC: U.S. Department of Health and Human Services Administration for Children and Families.

U.S. Department of Health and Human Services (HHS). (1996). *The third national inci-
    dence study of child abuse and neglect.* Washington, DC: U.S. Department of Health
    and Human Services, Administration for Children and Family.

U.S. Department of Health and Human Services (HHS). (1997). *National study of protec-
    tive, preventive and reunification services delivered to children and their families: Final
    report.* Washington, DC: U.S. Department of Health and Human Services, Adminis-
    tration for Children and Families.

U.S. General Accounting Office (GAO). (1989). *Foster parent recruiting and preservice
    training practices need evaluation.* Report to Congressional Requesters from Linda
    Morra, Director of Congressional Studies. GAOHRD-89-86 Washington, DC: Au-
    thor.

Veltkamp, L. J. & Miller, T. W. (1994). *Clinical handbook of child abuse and neglect.* Madi-
    son, CT: International Universities Press, Inc.

Walker, C. E., Bonner, B. L., & Kaufman, K. L. (1988). *The physically & sexually abused
    child.* New York: Pergammon.

Widom, C. S. & Ames, M. A. (1994). Criminal consequences of childhood sexual vic-
    timization. *Child Abuse and Neglect, 18*(4), 305–318.

Wirt, R. D., Lachar, D., Klinedinst, J. K., & Seat, P. D. (1984). *Multidimensional descrip-
    tion of child personality: A manual for the Personality Inventory for Children, revised
    1984.* Los Angeles, CA: Western Psychological Services.

Wolfe, V. V., Wolfe, D. A., Gentile, C. & LaRose, L. (1987). *Children's Impact of Traumatic
    Events Scale – revised.* Unpublished manuscript, University of Western Ontario at
    London, Ontario.

About the Author

Sally G. Hoyle, Ph.D., is a licensed psychologist and writer who specializes in assessment and treatment of children and families. Currently, Dr. Hoyle is project director of a research study on foster care. She lectures locally and nationally on child mental health topics and has a private practice in Beachwood, Ohio. She is also the author of *When Do I Go Home? Intervention Strategies for Foster Parents and Helping Professionals*, published by CWLA Press.